Lost... and Never Found

Anita Gustafson

SCHOLASTIC INC.
New York Toronto London Auckland Sydney Tokyo

ISBN 0-590-32980-4

Copyright © 1985 by Anita Gustafon. All rights reserved. Published by Scholastic Inc.

12 11 10 9 8 7 6 5 4 3 2   4 5 6 7 8 9/8

Printed in the U.S.A.   06

Contents

Introduction

Every year thousands of people disappear — old people, young people, children. They leave home in the same way they always have — to go to school or to work or to run an errand — but sometimes something strange happens. Sometimes — they don't come back.

Where do these people go? What happens to them?

Sometimes these questions can be answered. Some missing persons return on their own; many others are found by the police. The New York City Police Department's Bureau of Missing Persons, for example, has handled around 30,000 cases every year since it began in 1914, and most of the case files eventually closed because the people were found. But a handful of their case files remain open. These missing persons were never found — dead *or* alive. What happened to them is anybody's guess.

The stories in this book are about such mysterious, unsolved cases. They range from a man who simply melted away to the writer who laughed at the idea that such a thing could happen; from an explorer to a pair of possible spies; from an heiress who walked away from a fortune to a newspaper carrier who disappeared from his route.

Some of these cases are famous. Others, concerning people whose disappearances were not national news, are not so well known. But all of them have one thing in common — the people in them vanished without a trace. They were lost . . . and never found.

What happened to them?

Orion Williamson

One of the weirdest of all missing persons cases began in Alabama in 1854 on what seemed like an ordinary midsummer day. But something shockingly out of the ordinary would happen before that July morning was over — a young farmer named Orion Williamson would vanish in such a frightening way that his family and friends would never be able to understand or to accept what they themselves had seen!

Williamson and his wife were sitting on the porch of their Alabama farmhouse as they often did in the morning, talking quietly and watching their little boy play near them. From time to time, Williamson glanced at the horses that were grazing in a field across the yard. It was as lazy and peaceful a morning as always, and Williamson thought he had all the time in the world to get his chores done. But finally he stood and stretched, saying, "I think I'll bring the horses in."

His wife watched him as he ambled across the yard and into the field, saw him stoop to pick up a small stick and swish it idly in the drooping heads of the ankle-deep grass he passed through.

A horse-drawn buggy rattled along the road on the other side of the field, carrying Armour Wren and his son James home from Selma. When they saw Williamson walking toward them, they pulled their horse to a stop, and James stood in the buggy to wave. The Wrens weren't in any hurry this morning, either; they had time to visit with a neighbor.

And that's when it happened.

With the Wrens looking on from their buggy and his family watching from the porch, Orion Williamson vanished. One second he was walking through the field; the next second the field was empty.

Electrified, not believing what they had just witnessed, the Wrens jumped from their buggy and dashed across the field to meet Williamson's family on the spot where they had all last seen him.

He wasn't there, not even a trace of him; that much was apparent. Not only had *he* disappeared, but so had the stick and most of the grass that had been growing on that spot.

"It's impossible! Impossible!" Armour Wren cried, dropping to his knees. He couldn't see anything, but he must have thought it would be possible to feel something, because he kept running his hands feverishly over the earth, muttering "impossible" all the time.

But Wren felt nothing. There was nothing to feel; the ground wasn't disturbed. He saw no sign of a struggle, either. If someone or something had taken Williamson, it had done so easily and completely.

But he couldn't be gone! Even if he wasn't where they had last seen him, Williamson had to be somewhere. Anything else was impossible! So, for the next two hours, all four witnesses to Orion Williamson's disappearance searched the field with growing disbelief, confusion, and finally panic when their search produced absolutely nothing — no clues, no ideas, not a single link to him. Mrs. Williamson collapsed in shock.

When the Wrens took her to the hospital in Selma and explained what had caused her breakdown, the news flew around town, drawing three hundred men from their everyday occupations to an eerie new job — searching for a man who had suddenly, mysteriously, inexplicably vanished. The men rushed to the field and organized their search. They formed three rows an arm's length apart, then moved across the field inch by inch, laboriously examining the ground, stooping to brush their fingers through the grass to overturn each stone. They fine-combed the field all afternoon, until it must have seemed to them that they had touched and examined every square inch of land — to no avail.

Even when night fell they persisted, carrying torches and calling for bloodhounds to help in the search. The keen-nosed dogs took the scent from some of Williamson's clothes and snuffled off on his trail. All night the men searched by the light of their flaring torches, behind their increasingly confused and frustrated dogs.

By morning, news of the disappearance had spread for miles around Selma, and the searchers had company. Hundreds of curious onlookers came, most of them feeling alarmed as they whispered questions to one another. But some of them had explanations for what had happened, which they were happy to share with anyone who cared to listen: "The man has to be there somewhere. Why, sure. Fella can't just disappear! He's fallen down a hidden well, sure as I'm standing here . . . or been buried in a cave-in. You take my word for it!"

Could Williamson be found beneath the soil of the field? Was the land unstable and shifting, the kind that would be likely to cave in? A geologist with a team of experts arrived, and they dug to find the answers to those questions. They discovered a solid sheet of limestone bedrock underlying the field, and they didn't find any forgotten wells or camouflaged crevices or man-swallowing sinkholes.

By now newspaper reporters had heard about what had happened to Williamson, and it sounded like such an incredible story that they swarmed to the field. All their articles were essentially the same: A strange thing has happened — a man has "vanished into thin air," as the old saying goes. Some of the reporters found themselves suggesting to their readers that there might be some truth to that old saying; others stuck to hard facts. But whether the stories were factual or philosophical, in the end all of them made the same bald statements — no one had found Williamson, apparently no one could, and the search was being abandoned.

Finally, after several weeks, the search *was* given up officially, but that didn't stop curious people from gathering. As late as the following spring, visitors were still coming to gape at the field where Orion Williamson had disappeared and to shake their heads in amazed disbelief.

Some of those people weren't ready to give up the "investigation," and they noticed something new about the field. On the spot where Williamson had vanished was a circle of dead grass about fifteen feet across. When they pointed this out to Mrs. Williamson, her reaction was strange. She seemed terrified!

"I don't want to talk about it," she said,

but the questions kept coming at her until finally she did break down and talk, and what she said was almost as unbelievable as what had happened to her husband.

She didn't want to talk about his disappearance, she said, because her husband had not completely disappeared!

She claimed that although Williamson was "invisible," his voice had stayed behind. It called for help from the circle of dead grass. Mrs. Williamson and her son listened to it for two weeks. The voice grew weaker each day. Finally, it became a mere whisper, a "death whisper" — and soon it stopped completely. Nothing was left of Williamson at all.

Eventually people stopped bothering Mrs. Williamson with a lot of little questions, but they still wanted to know the answer to the big one: What happened to Orion Williamson?

The writer Ambrose Bierce was intrigued by the question. He interviewed some of the search party who had failed to find Williamson, and he studied the grassy, treeless field from which the man had disappeared. Obviously he hadn't been able to hide behind a tree and slip away when no one was looking, and, according to the geologists' report, it was equally obvious that he had not somehow been buried beneath that field. But there had to be some reasonable explanation, Bierce thought. There *had* to be. A person "evaporating"? How could such a thing happen?

Bierce was so interested that he continued his investigation and consulted a German scientist who specialized in the study of fantastic events, such as people vanishing into thin air. In fact, this scientist had written a book about incredible happenings and had a theory about what might have happened to Williamson.

The young farmer, he suggested, had walked into a "void spot of universal ether." He explained that these void spots were short-lived, lasting only a few seconds, but they were immensely strong — able to completely destroy any solid objects such as grass or people that happened to be in them. The searchers who had combed the field had been saved from Williamson's fate because, by the time they got there, the void spot had vanished.

Another scientist had a different idea. He thought Williamson had walked into a "magnetic field." Like void spots, magnetic fields were momentary but powerful; walking into one would completely disintegrate a person. If that's what had happened to Williamson, this scientist went on, the very atoms of his body had been rearranged. According to his theory, Orion Williamson had walked into a magnetic field and had been hurled — in a different form — into another dimension.

No one could *see* anything that was in this other dimension, but people could occasionally *hear* sounds coming from there, which was why Mrs. Williamson had been able to hear what she called his "death whispers."

Neither explanation seemed satisfactory to Bierce, and he wrote a story in which he dismissed both the scientists' explanations and anyone who believed them. Undoubtedly he would have scoffed at later claims that Williamson was picked up by a UFO, too. (Strangely enough, Bierce would disappear years later. His story is in the next chapter.)

So the big question remained unanswered. What *did* happen to Orion Williamson?

No one knows.

But what happened to him isn't the only confusion connected with his disappearance. Years later, a newspaper reporter added another strange twist. The reporter was looking for a good story and a fast paycheck, so he took the facts from the Orion Williamson case and made up a whole new cast of characters. He named *his* disappearing man David Lang, and he moved the story from Selma, Alabama, to Gallatin, Tennessee, and from 1854 to 1880. His "report" was a huge success! In fact, it was reprinted so often in so many places that today, David Lang is a name known by many people, whereas few have heard of Orion Williamson. It's as if

Orion Williamson had been born only to disappear — twice!

It's that double oblivion that makes his story unique. How do people "vanish into thin air"? No one knows. Except perhaps Orion Williamson. . . .

Ambrose Bierce

Ambrose Bierce was sixteen when he had a terrifying nightmare.

He was wandering in an unfamiliar place, a blasted and forbidding plain, stumbling on and on until suddenly his path was blocked by a massive building. He went in and found himself in a large room. The room wasn't empty; it contained a bed. And Bierce wasn't alone; someone was lying on the bed. As is the way in dreams, he knew instantly that the body was dead, and he was afraid. But he felt compelled to approach the bedside anyway.

The corpse was dreadfully decomposed. It was shocking — its face black, its lips stretched in a grotesque grin, and its eyes sealed shut forever.

But as he stood there, the eyes began to open, slowly and inexorably. He drew back in horror, but found he couldn't run, could not even tear his gaze away. As if hypnotized, he watched the living eyes widen in the rotten flesh. Wider and wider they opened until they were fully aware and sentient. That's when the second and more mind-numbing shock struck Bierce.

The dead man's eyes were clear and blue. They were knowingly sardonic. They were Bierce's own!

The dreadful truth burst upon him Bierce himself was the rotting corpse; he himself, its only mourner.

Such nightmares seemed to haunt Bierce's life, spilling over into what he wrote. He was obsessed by the thought of death; many of his stories end unsettlingly at the side of a grave.

Death was his biggest fascination, but he had others. He was also drawn to weird and unexplainable events, such as Orion Williamson's disappearance. Bierce turned up at the scene of more than one such real-life mystery to investigate and write a report; his reports are gathered in books such as *Fantastic Fables* and *Can Such Things Be?*

Sometimes he was terse and scoffing about the strange events. He laughed at Orion Williamson's disappearance, saying it was surrounded by the "most monstrous and grotesque fictions." Bierce simply couldn't buy everything he heard about the Williamson case. He concluded his report on it by saying

13

all that could be known for sure about this disappearance was what had been accepted into evidence in court when Williamson's estate was settled.

Some of his other reports, however, end on a curious note of wonderment, as if Bierce wanted to disbelieve the facts in a case, but couldn't.

One of these reports was called "The Thing at Nolan," and it was about what happened to a Missouri man named Charles May. May was pleasant; he had "a sunny, jovial disposition." His son John was the exact opposite, with a "morose and surly" disposition and a quick, violent temper. One day in the heat of an argument Charles struck his son. It was completely out of character for him to do that, and he apologized instantly. John wouldn't forgive him, instead growling a threat: "You will die for that." Time went on with no decrease in John's hostility, and one day when his father left the house, John picked up a shovel and followed him. John returned; his father didn't. Soon after that John came down with a "brain fever," during which he raved incoherently about killing someone. Nobody knew what he was talking about. True, his father was gone, but John wouldn't kill his own father! Would he? Of course not! And anyway, no body had been found. . . .

Then came some startling news — Charles May had appeared at the front door of a store in Nolan, a small town eight miles away from where the family lived. He walked through the place stiffly and silently and strangely, and left by the back door. The usually genial man had said nothing, had greeted no one in the place. But none of his friends was surprised about that because they were too astonished at May's appearance. A deep gash split the whole left side of his face and neck, and blood had spread and stained his light-gray shirt. May was seriously injured! Had he been in a fight? He must have been, his friends thought, and that was unusual, too. They were sure the man had gone to wash off the blood in the brook in back, and they waited for him to return, but he never did. Charles May had disappeared again!

John May was put on trial for the murder of his missing father, but was acquitted for lack of evidence. If a body could not be found, murder could not be proven. Immediately after the trial, he moved from the area, and the rest of the May family soon tired of gawkers and questions and left, too.

Then, several months later, Charles May's body was discovered. Astonishingly, his body bore *exactly the same wounds described by the people in the store in Nolan!* By his side lay the murder weapon — a bloody shovel. John *had* killed his father!

But the way Bierce's report read, he wasn't greatly interested in John's guilt or innocence. What captured his attention was the question of what had stalked grimly and silently through the store at Nolan.

Did Bierce honestly think that a person could rise from the grave to give mute testimony to his shocking murder? Did he want to believe that people could vanish into thin air?

Whether or not he believed, his reports certainly drew attention to such events and caused other people to think about the unthinkable. More important, whether or not Bierce believed in mysterious disappearances, the *idea* of vanishing intrigued him greatly.

He began to joke about the possibility of his own disappearance, and in 1913 he set out on a journey that would make all his jokes a reality. He would never return home from that trip, but would disappear as completely as Orion Williamson had — as if the earth had swallowed him up.

Still, there was a difference. Unlike Orion Williamson, Ambrose Bierce *planned* to disappear. And, unlike the thousands of missing persons who walk away quietly every year, Bierce made no secret of his plans. He was going to visit the battlefields of the Civil War, then continue on to Mexico and South America. He would cross the Andes, and he would keep on going.

Bierce wrote letters to his family and friends before he left to tell them his plans, say good-bye, and clear up odds and ends of unfinished business. In one letter, a farewell to his daughter, Bierce said that he'd transferred the ownership of his cemetery lot to her. He didn't want it, he said, because he didn't want her to have to be "bothered about the mortal part of your daddy." Bierce planned a smooth and irrevocable exit, and that — by and large — is what he achieved.

On October 2, 1913, after his visit to the Civil War battlefields, Bierce left his home in Washington to carry out his plans. He stopped in New Orleans, then went on to El Paso, Texas, where he crossed the border into Juarez, Mexico. On December 26, 1913, he sent a letter to his secretary from Chihuahua, Mexico. That was the last time anyone heard from Ambrose Bierce.

What happened to him?

Bierce himself had few doubts about what would happen. He thought he would die on this trip, and he was probably right.

Look at the facts as Bierce himself would have — full in the face and with no sentimentality:

• He was seventy-one years old.

• He suffered from acute asthmatic seizures during which he had to gasp and struggle for breath.

• He was leaving for what he called " 'strange countries,' in which things happen."

He wrote "strange countries," but he probably specifically meant Mexico, which was in the midst of a bloody revolution at the time. Pancho Villa, a onetime bandit, was leading a revolt against the government of dictator Victoriano Huerta.

In his final letters, Bierce claimed he was "dressed for death" and "sleepy for death." He wrote to a friend that he'd hate it if he died quietly "between sheets," and he ended roundly, "God willing, I won't." He wrote: "If you hear of my being stood up against a Mexican stone wall and shot to rags, please know that I think that a pretty good way to depart this life. It beats old age, disease, and falling down the cellar stairs."

No, Bierce had very little doubt about what would happen to him in war-torn Mexico.

He knew the danger of entering a battle zone because he knew what war was like. Decades earlier, when President Lincoln put out his first call for volunteers for the Union army, eighteen-year-old Bierce responded immediately. He enlisted in the 9th Indiana Regiment for the usual term of three months — that was as long as anyone expected this little civil quarrel to last. The volunteers were sent to Virginia, and young Bierce proved himself under fire, once fearlessly rescuing a wounded comrade. When his first term of enlistment came to an end and the Civil War didn't, Bierce "reupped" and was made a sergeant of volunteers.

His war record was one to be proud of, if — as Bierce would point out — anyone could be proud of war. He survived the most deadly action of the war, including bloody Shiloh, where for two days in April, 1862, the quiet meadow whined with bullets, and the stench of fear and death filled the soft spring air. Then came Murfreesboro and Chickamauga and Chattanooga and the capture of Atlanta and, finally, Sherman's march to the sea.

Cantankerous, tough Union General William Babcock Hazen liked what he saw of the gritty teenager. He promoted Bierce to first lieutenant, assigning him to the highly dangerous prebattle duty of scouting and mapmaking. It was solitary duty, undertaken with no hope of help if captured.

When the Civil War was over, Hazen kept in touch with Bierce. He waited for him to recover from a head wound, then arranged to bring him West to help tame that still wild territory.

There is absolutely no doubt that when the aging Bierce left for Mexico years later, he knew he was setting out on what he called a *"jornada de muerte"* — a journey of death. He went willingly and happily. "To be a gringo in Mexico," he wrote, "that is indeed euthanasia." Euthanasia — a mercy killing, a merciful death.

Once across the border and into Juarez, which had recently been liberated by Villa, Bierce went even further. Not content to be merely ready and waiting for death, Bierce seemed to go forward eagerly to find it. He accepted credentials that would allow him to accompany Villa's army. Bierce was now seventy-two years old, and he hadn't been on a horse for thirty years. He said in his last letter, however, that he'd ridden four miles to mail it, and that the next day, he would ride with Villa's army for Ojinaga, a city under siege.

Being at war apparently agreed with Bierce, even though he never wrote about war's glory. Looking for death seemed to invigorate him, to give him new life. Bierce was a contradictory, complicated man.

He was born July 24, 1842, the youngest of a family of eight children raised on a primitive Ohio farm. He parents were rigid people who took care to explain hellfire and damnation thoroughly to their children. According to biographers, Ambrose was the only Bierce who managed to escape his family. He did it, psychologists claim, by becoming fiercely independent, an attitude that would continue the rest of his life.

Bierce was a satirist — a comedian with more on his mind than a couple of laughs. A satirist wants to change the world, and on at least one occasion, Bierce's satire worked spectacularly well. Almost single-handedly, he stopped a federal treasury "raid" connived at by one of the "robber baron" railroad owners of the times.

That probably made Bierce happy for a few minutes, but most of the time he was bitter. In fact, a lot of people called him "Bitter" Bierce.

A lot of people also wondered why Bierce behaved the way he did. Sometimes he just wasn't quite nice.

For example, even though he continually thought about death, he didn't seem to know how a civilized, normal person was supposed to deal with death. He wouldn't allow tombstones to be placed on the graves of his wife and two sons. People thought that was a little peculiar.

And when Day, one of his sons, killed himself, Bierce went down to the morgue and identified the body lying on the slab. So far, so good. But then he pulled himself erect and shouted at his dead son, "You're a noble soul, Day — you did just right." Definitely peculiar!

And he had the body of his other son, Leigh, cremated. So far, so good. But then he kept the ashes in a cigar box on his desk. A cigar box! To make matters worse, he occasionally tapped his burning cigars into the same box!

"Why do you act like that?" people asked him.

"Nothing matters," Bierce replied, meaning that none of the rules of society really mattered to him. He thought they were silly. His bleak childhood may have inspired his disregard for living "right," or it may have grown from his disillusionment at the Civil War's corrupt aftermath. Whatever the reason, the way Bierce behaved wasn't the way polite society expected any normal person to behave.

And his bizarre tales of the macabre were at odds with how people were expected to think. In "A Man with Two Lives," for example, the hero, soldier David William Duck, is killed, scalped, mutilated, and buried. It is a rough day for Duck, but he wakes up that night refreshed and heads back to Fort C. F. Smith. There, he's understandably confused when others tell him he's dead. What's more, they tell him how he died! They give Duck his papers and the clothing he was wearing when he died, then throw him into the guardhouse as an impostor. He escapes and attempts to find his death site. He can't. Now commonly known as "Dead Duck," he remains confused about what happened to him, even though he realizes that — somehow — he defeated death.

By the 1890s, disturbing stories like these had made Bierce's name a household word, and everything seemed to be going Bierce's way. He was rakishly handsome, with bright golden hair and a flowing mustache. He had a devil-may-care attitude toward society's rules. But he was hardworking and conscientious about things he thought mattered.

He was the acknowledged leader of West Coast writers, San Francisco's "literary lion."

But Bierce's fame was an up-and-down thing. He was forgotten, then "discovered" so many times that he must have felt invisible even before he actually disappeared. Of course, there were reasons why people forgot him so often. He didn't act "right." Who knew what he was going to do or say next?

Years had passed like this and by the time Bierce announced his intention to create and enact a final disappearance, no one tried to stop him. Some people knew they couldn't; he'd do what he pleased. Others — those who had been on the stinging end of his satiric barbs — probably didn't want to.

But lots of people had ideas about what actually happened to Ambrose Bierce when he didn't come back from his journey of death.

Some explanations of his disappearance point to his last letter, when he wrote that he was going with Villa's army to Ojinaga. The seige of that city began on January 11, 1914, and one Mexican army dispatch lists a casualty named A. Pierce. Was that Ambrose *Bierce?* It's an easy enough spelling mistake to make.

If so, was he killed in action?

Or had he simply collapsed in the lung-choking dust during the siege, fighting at the end the asthmatic's unsuccessful struggle for the breath of life?

Another explanation recognizes Bierce's unique personality and accepts the rumor that Bierce fell into an argument with Villa, during which he shouted, "You're nothing but a bandit!" and threatened to go over to the enemy. This theory goes that Villa listened, then merely shrugged. What could a general do in such a case? Ask his personal executioner to do him a favor, of course. Villa did. The executioner complied. Bierce died.

Another version of this explanation has it that after Villa shrugged he forgot all about Bierce's threat to change his allegiance. Bierce didn't, however, and he was shot while running machine guns to the enemy.

None of these explanations can be substantiated. No one knows which of them is most true . . . or even if any of them is true at all.

Some other answers to the mystery of Bierce's disappearance surfaced later.

One claim was that Bierce never even left home, but is buried in his own backyard, after either being poisoned or poisoning himself.

Another had Bierce leaving home, but not following his announced itinerary. Bierce, according to this theory, went instead to the Grand Canyon, where he raised a pistol to his head and pulled the trigger, tumbling to lie forever in the unmarked grave he seemed to want so much.

Still another idea is that Bierce went to Mexico but didn't stay with Villa for long. He set out for South America, and some wild, primitive tribe of natives in southern Mexico found the old man wandering around. They boiled him alive and put his shrunken remains into a big bottle. Then they worshipped the little man in the large bottle. Well . . . stranger things have happened. Bierce would be the first to recognize that.

What *really* happened to Ambrose Bierce to put an end to his famous journey of death? No one knows. And that's exactly the way Bierce would have wanted it.

Dorothy Arnold

Dorothy Arnold's life appeared to be an easy, smooth routine.

In the morning she went shopping in the better establishments along Fifth Avenue in New York City.

She lunched quietly at noon with other girls of her class. Many of them could trace their families clear back to the *Mayflower;* all of them had been socially prominent for generations. She herself was a 1905 graduate of Bryn Mawr, a college for women located on a spacious eighty-one acre campus near Philadelphia.

At night, she went to debutante balls. She had been introduced to society for several years now, and her younger sister would make her debut soon. They were both heiresses to the fortune accumulated by their father's importing business, Francis R. Arnold & Company.

Morning, noon, and night — this is what she did to occupy her time, every day.

Well, *almost* every day. Some days she wrote stories, and some days she spent with George — but no one was supposed to know about that! And, thank heaven, no one seemed to. At any rate, Mother and Father didn't, and they were the important ones. Along with Uncle Rufus, of course, who was United States Supreme Court Justice Rufus Peckham.

She sometimes wondered what they would say if they knew. But they didn't, and they would never find out. She was handling everything quite capably.

On December 12, 1910, she set out on a shopping trip, saying that she wanted to find a dress to wear at her younger sister's debut. It appeared to be just another routine day. But that day would be anything but routine for Dorothy. Today she would shatter her routine forever. Today she would disappear.

December 12th started out routinely enough. Dorothy awakened at the usual hour in her room in her parent's impressive and stately home at 108 East 79th Street. She dressed with her usual care in her usual handsome and expensive clothes. Garments, her mother called them.

She hooked the buttons on her high-topped, suede shoes. She lifted her hat — a fashionable Baker chapeau, with a wide, black-velvet brim and a crown piled high with artificial roses — and nestled it on top of her crimped hair. She slipped into her hip-length coat. It was trimmed on the bottom with fringe that danced as she walked.

She loved to walk, even though all the best shops were offering bright-colored dresses with narrow hems. Hobble skirts, they were called, so narrow that they allowed you to take steps no longer than two or three inches. A longer stride would split the skirt, so the shops recommended that a braid restraint be worn just below the knees to keep you from stepping out! Those hobble skirts weren't for Dorothy Arnold, not this morning. She planned to cover a lot of distance — over five miles — and she couldn't do that by inching along.

At last nearly ready to set out, Dorothy checked inside her satin clutchbag to make sure the thirty-six dollars she'd recently withdrawn from her bank account was there. Then, tucking one hand into the soft, satin lining of her silver-fox muff, she left.

It was eleven o'clock, a decent hour of the morning for proper, socially prominent, single girls to be out and about during these Edwardian times.

The day was cold, but strong and heavy-set Dorothy briskly walked the nearly two miles to her first stop — Park and Tilford's at 58th

Street. There she selected a box of chocolates, charged the purchase to her family's account, and took it with her.

Her next stop was Brentano's bookstore on 27th Street, another sizable distance. She stopped to talk with friends, other society girls who were out and about doing their shopping.

In Brentano's, she found a copy of the book she wanted and took that with her, too. She was carrying *An Engaged Girl's Sketches,* by Emily Calvin Blake, when she left the bookshop and ran into her friend Gladys King. They talked a few minutes about Dorothy's sister's upcoming debut, then waved good-bye, and Dorothy walked across Fifth Avenue.

Whatever her destination that morning, when Dorothy left her friend and crossed Fifth Avenue, she walked into oblivion. Her mysterious disappearance is one of the most famous and baffling missing-persons cases of all times.

But at first, only her immediate family knew she was gone. Alarmed when Dorothy didn't return home that evening, her parents quietly telephoned friends to make well-bred inquiries.

But no one had seen their daughter after Gladys King watched her cross Fifth Avenue and merge with the dense crowd of pedestrians hurrying along there.

Even though they were growing more and

more anxious and worried, the Arnolds hesitated to call the police immediately. To do so seemed a bit rash, they thought. Their social position guaranteed that the first hint of Dorothy's disappearance would release a flood of reporters. None of the Arnolds felt up to being gaped at or questioned at the moment. In any case, calling the police immediately also seemed a bit premature. Dorothy might return on her own any minute now.

And if she did, one could only hope she had some reasonable explanation for her rude and inconsiderate behavior!

If she didn't, of course, that would be dreadful. Perhaps there was someone else they could call on for help, the Arnolds thought. Someone whom they could rely on to be discreet. Someone who understood the situation, their position.

The Arnolds decided to speak to their attorney, John S. Keith. He had often escorted Dorothy to social functions, and he could be trusted with this delicate matter.

For weeks, Keith quietly searched the cities in which he and the Arnolds thought Dorothy might be found. She was familiar with Philadelphia, Boston, and New York, so they were the most likely places for her to have gone. The wealthy Arnolds hadn't received any ransom demands, so they didn't think their daughter had been kidnapped.

But she might have had an accident; somebody may have harmed her for the money in her clutchbag. Thirty-six dollars wasn't a fortune even in 1910, but it was still more than twice the average weekly wage of fifteen dollars at that time. Keith visited morgues, prisons, and hospitals; talked with police, patients, prisoners — anyone who might have even a scrap of information about the missing girl in the Baker chapeau. He was both relieved and worried when he failed to find any trace of her.

The Arnolds called in other private investigators who could be expected to proceed with decorum. At one point, they even summoned the famous Pinkerton National Detective Agency, whose motto was "We Never Sleep." It could have been "We Never Give Up," because Pinkerton operatives tracked down outlaws such as Frank and Jesse James, the Younger Brothers, the Reno Brothers, and Butch Cassidy and the Sundance Kid after years of searching. These desperados knew how to disappear and hide, and the Pinkertons found them. Dorothy Arnold was a rank amateur at getting lost, but her disappearance foiled Pinkerton's best efforts.

Six weeks passed, and now there was no other reasonable option for the Arnolds. There was nothing else they could do except tell the police. The Arnolds did, calling a formal press conference as well. Publicity couldn't be avoided now, but they thought maybe they could control what the press was told.

The reporters were happy to get the story. 1910 had been a bad year for stop-the-press news, and the first weeks of 1911 weren't much better. What could you say about 1910? Fuller Brush became a corporation. So what? The Boy Scouts and the Camp Fire Girls had been founded. That was nice, but hardly a screaming headline. Sure, there'd been a little excitement when women got the vote in Washington State, what with all the suffragettes marching up and down and making general nuisances of themselves, and there were all those heart-tugging stories they had written last summer about the first Father's Day. None of that was much to hang a whole year of daily papers on! But this, now — this looked good. This smelled like a real story!

"Had Dorothy ever disappeared before?" a reporter asked.

Mrs. Arnold replied in the crisp, ladylike tone that had always before quelled such impertinent nonsense. "Indeed not," she said. "Dorothy is not in the habit of disappearing. She led a restricted, controlled life with no men in it."

Mr. Arnold scowled. He had information he hadn't shared with his wife yet. She didn't know about George, that — that *playboy!*

A reporter looked him square in the eye and asked, "Do you object to your daughter keeping company with men?"

Mr. Arnold drilled his reply straight at the brash reporter. It wasn't true he objected to having men call at the house for Dorothy. In fact, he would have been very happy if she had associated more with young men than she did. Especially, he said, gathering steam and emotion, he would have liked Dorothy to associate with some young men with brains and position, with professions and businesses that kept them occupied.

Dorothy's father was scowling about George Griscom, Jr. George was forty-two years old, but he wanted people to call him Junior. He was unmarried and wealthy, and he had taken several secret trips to Boston with twenty-five-year-old Dorothy — at Dorothy's expense. One time, their trip was so expensive that Dorothy had to pawn some of her jewelry to pay their hotel bill. But that was nothing to Dorothy; she was apparently passionately and desperately in love with Junior — and had been for a couple of years.

Always she had come home from their rendezvous and resumed the "restricted, controlled life" of which her mother was so proud. No one knew about her temporary lapses from the kind of conduct expected of an Edwardian girl of social standing.

Now Dorothy's father ended his answer

abruptly and angrily. "I don't approve of young men who have nothing to do." That's all he would say about the subject of men.

He was willing to talk about another topic, however — his daughter's interest in writing. He'd discuss it, but he was pretty embarrassed about it. It was obvious he thought her writing was a romantic notion, a silly girl's ridiculous idea. He admitted that he had once found some of her short stories hidden in her bedroom.

"Were the stories any good?" a reporter asked.

"Drivel, that's all," Arnold said, shaking his head.

"Are you going to release those stories?"

"No," Arnold said shortly.

"But, sir —"

Arnold interrupted. "I burned them," he said, making it obvious that he'd burn them again if he could.

Dorothy had sent two stories, "Poinsettia Flames" and "Lotus Leaves," to *McClure's Magazine. McClure's* shot them back by return mail. Laying aside her rejected stories, Dorothy had written this note to herself: "*McClure's* has turned me down. Failure stares me in the face. All I can see ahead is a long road with no turning. Mother will always think it was an accident."

Mother will always think it was an accident. Later historians and detectives alike would ask what she'd meant by that. Whatever the meaning of her cryptic note, Dorothy's family teased her pitilessly about her writing. She endured it, one day mentioning to her father that she might move to Greenwich Village to pursue her literary career. "I forbid you to leave home," he declared. "A good writer can write anywhere!"

Now, as he continued to field the reporter's questions, Mr. Arnold still thought that if you were any good, you could write anywhere.

The press conference ended and the story broke in the papers. It was a great story, and it wasn't long before reporters uncovered more of it. They broke the news about Dorothy's secret affair with George Griscom. The scandal rocked society.

Griscom, who had run for Florence, Italy, when he sensed his involvement in the Dorothy Arnold disappearance would soon hit the headlines, cabled back immediately. He insisted that he didn't have the slightest idea where Dorothy was.

Reporters asked the Arnolds what they had to say about that. Mr. Arnold had little to say, and Mrs. Arnold wasn't around to say even that much. She had gone to a country estate to ease her worries about Dorothy, Arnold told reporters.

Mrs. Arnold had gone away to ease her worries, but she wasn't at a country estate. She'd gone to Florence because she was sure she'd find Dorothy somewhere in the vicinity of George Griscom. She took her son John with her in case she needed help handling George.

But even after John threatened to "soundly thrash" him, Griscom could produce nothing of Dorothy but her love letters. He handed over a packet of these that spanned two years' time, once again swearing he didn't know where Dorothy was. The love letters didn't offer a hint of where she might have run away to.

Mrs. Arnold and John came home from their secret mission, and the Arnold family issued posters through the New York Police Department that carried Dorothy's picture and home address. Griscom returned to the United States soon and lost no time in placing dutifully desperate "Come Home" ads in newspapers.

But Dorothy didn't come home to George; nor did she respond to her parents' posters. Her disappearance became international news; people all over the world followed the latest developments with increasing puzzlement.

In England, a twenty-year-old woman read the accounts with much more than casual interest. For more than ten years afterward, this woman was obsessed with the fate of an American girl she felt she understood. They had a lot in common, she thought. And she would herself disappear for a short time before she came home and began to write her own stories. She wrote mysteries — what else? — and her name was Agatha Christie.

Meanwhile in the United States, mail responding to the ads and the posters poured in. Even though police could see no further trail, thousands of private citizens claimed to know the whereabouts of the missing heiress. Someone claimed that Dorothy was in a small Mexican town, drugged and powerless against the wishes of the white-slavers who held her captive. Someone else claimed that Dorothy was in Hawaii, happily strolling the Honolulu beaches with a handsome young man. Dorothy Arnold was reported to have been seen in more than one hundred different cities, but when the reports were checked out one by one, every identification proved false.

There was no way to check some of the reports. When a person claimed that on the very day Dorothy disappeared, a white swan materialized out of nowhere and began to swim in the Central Park lagoon, there wasn't much police could do. They just listened as politely as possible as this person explained that Dorothy had left an unhappy human life to take up the free existence of a beautiful bird.

What happened to her?

Most people wanted to help answer that question, but no one really knew.

Then, six years after she vanished, it appeared that someone might know. A new installment of the Dorothy Arnold story broke in the papers when a Rhode Island convict issued a press release claiming that he'd been paid $150 to dig a grave for the missing heiress. Who had paid him? A young man of great wealth, the convict said, and the description of that young man coincided to a remarkable extent with that of George Griscom, Jr. Dorothy died following a "secret operation," according to this man, and he'd dug her grave in the dark of night in the cellar of a house near West Point.

Police dug up a lot of West Point cellars, but the remains of Dorothy Arnold weren't in any of them. The mystery of her disappearance continued, and still no one really knew where she might be.

Then, eleven years after she disappeared, it again appeared that someone else might know. Police Captain John H. Ayers, then newly appointed head of New York City's Missing Persons Bureau, was speaking before a group of high school students. He claimed that police had known the answer to the mystery for years. Everyone immediately asked him to explain himself, of course, but Ayers suddenly decided not to.

Did the police really know the fate of Dorothy Arnold? Or had Captain Ayers only felt as if he were on the spot and said what he did to impress his audience?

Although no one could say for sure what

happened to Dorothy, there were a lot of explanations for what might have happened to her.

One of the most long-lived of these explanations is that she had indeed had a "secret operation" — an abortion. Because abortion was illegal in 1910, the only place she could go was to a back-alley quack. According to the people who hold this theory, instead of shopping for a dress for her younger sister's debut on December 12th, Dorothy Arnold died on an operating table, and her body was disposed of in panicked secrecy.

Another explanation also takes into account Dorothy's relationship with Griscom. This idea, however, maintains that the publicity-conscious Arnolds discovered her condition and sent her away to Switzerland, where they forced her to live a life of penance for her sins, alone in a remote chalet.

Yet another theory also relies on the theme of unhappy love. This one claims that Griscom, not returning Dorothy's feelings in the same manner and degree, refused to marry her. Dorothy, not being able to face life without marriage to Griscom, refused to live. According to this theory, Dorothy committed suicide by hurling herself down in some place where her body would be perfectly hidden for all time.

These last three explanations rely on the destructive power of thwarted romances and unrequited love. All of them are plausible, especially if Dorothy had nothing else on her mind except George.

But, in fact, she was unhappy about something else. Something that made her feel as if failure stared her in the face. Something about which she would do something that Mother would "always think . . . was an accident." She was unhappy that *McClure's Magazine* had rejected her stories.

And, in fact, Dorothy was unhappy at home; so unhappy she'd thought of leaving for Greenwich Village and a writing career. She'd even broached the subject to her dogmatic father, and he'd forbidden it, telling her with cruel insensitivity that a good writer could write anywhere. His implication was, of course, that he thought Dorothy was a rotten writer and that she would be a rotten writer no matter where she lived.

Did Dorothy Arnold silently rebel from the routine pattern of her constrained life at this point? After all, she'd had an education, and the suffragettes were saying that it was all right for women to take control of their lives. Did she take getaway money from her bank account and walk strongly and briskly into the crowds on Fifth Avenue, determined to make her father eat his words?

It's possible.

It's also possible that she had every intention of buying a debut dress, but as she walked in the crowds, her mind snapped.

There are cases in which a person simply steps from one life to another in mid-stride. These people have no memory of the life they left. If there are curious blanks in the early years of the new life they have picked up . . . well, they soon find themselves knowing how it *must* have been.

In any missing-persons case, any fate is possible.

Dorothy's mother and father spent more than $100,000 in futile attempts to find her. Finally they decided what her fate must have been. When they died, both their wills contained the same line: "I have made no provision for my beloved daughter, Dorothy H. C. Arnold, as I am satisfied that she is not alive."

Dorothy Arnold was lost . . . and never found.

Amelia Earhart

Commander Thompson was tense.

At 2:45 A.M., the voice of the famous American pilot had piped through the crackling static on wavelength 3105 into the radio room of the U.S. Coast Guard cutter *Itasca*. "Cloudy and overcast," she said, ". . . headwinds." Thompson immediately flashed a message to San Francisco: "*Itasca* heard Earhart plane at 0248."

But he expected Amelia Earhart to signal again at 3:15, and she didn't and he was getting tenser by the moment. She wasn't following the transmission schedule!

At 3:30 Thompson decided not to take the chance of losing contact. He broke the schedule himself. He radioed Earhart, transmitting the weather report to KHAQQ, Earhart's call letters. He added: "What is your position, KHAQQ? *Itasca* has heard your phone. Please go ahead on key. Acknowledge this broadcast next schedule."

At 3:45 Amelia Earhart signaled again: "*Itasca* from Earhart . . . *Itasca* from Earhart . . . overcast . . . will listen in on hour and half hour at 3105." She didn't acknowledge Thompson's message or give her position, and her voice sounded even farther away than before.

Thompson's radiomen called again and again, each time asking for the plane's position. AE signaled on schedule, but her faint-voiced messages came through garbled by static. They were fragmentary, and she never gave one bit of information about her position.

Frustration and anxiety in the cutter's radio room mounted. What was wrong? Why wouldn't AE give them her position? Didn't she know? Worse yet, couldn't she hear them? They *had* to know where she was!

The whole world was watching this flight, and they were responsible for bringing Amelia Earhart and her navigator Fred Noonan down safely on Howland Island, a tiny speck of land in the vast Pacific Ocean. The radio link was vital — and it didn't seem to be working!

Thompson was worried, but he steadied himself, told himself to stop it. After all, Earhart was one of the finest pilots who ever flew. She'd broken long-distance flight records, performed wonders in the air, pulled herself and her planes out of perilous situations, and walked away grinning. And Noonan was a pro. He knew the Pacific skies better than anyone else.

But Thompson was still worried. He knew there were just too many things that could go wrong. Noonan's navigational systems, for one thing. Both the gyro and the magnetic compasses could easily go haywire. Simply hanging a mechanical pencil or another metal object near the magnetic compass could cause the needle to veer from north and home in on that object. If that happened, Earhart and Noonan would be forced to use the stars for guidance. *That* would be impossible if skies were overcast, and Earhart had said they were.

There were no stars. . . .

Thompson felt a cold rush of fear. If Earhart and Noonan were flying through the night guided only by dead reckoning, the aircraft could be thrown hopelessly off course by even so much as one degree of deviation from flight plan. Each degree would send the plane a mile off course for every sixty miles of headway. Earhart's twin-engined Electra, specially built by Lockheed, would head out over thousands of miles of open sea. She'd never make it to Howland.

The *Itasca*'s radio operators shared Thompson's unease. They hung over their equipment, waiting for AE to signal.

Finally, at 6:15, her voice came through clearly. "About 100 miles out," she said, and the men in the radio room relaxed. The flight was going well after all, even if they couldn't get a bearing on the Electra's location. They calculated the time the plane should land, making allowances for the difference caused by the International Date Line that ran between AE's takeoff point in New Guinea and Howland. A little before 8 A.M., they thought; that's when you'd have to be on deck to see the Electra coming in!

But at 7:42 A.M., Amelia's frantic voice came through loud and clear, shattering that hopeful calculation. She was almost shouting: "KHAQQ calling *Itasca*. We must be on you but cannot see you. Gas is running low. Only about thirty minutes left. Been unable to reach you by radio. We are flying at an altitude of one thousand feet."

And fifteen minutes later, her voice came again, the loudest and clearest it had been and now even more alarmed. "KHAQQ calling *Itasca*. We are circling but cannot see you. Go ahead on seventy-five hundred either now or on schedule," she cried.

Thompson immediately ordered a steady stream of signals on the Morse direction-finding signal on seventy-five hundred kilocycles. For the first time, Amelia acknowledged the transmission. "We are receiving your signals," she said, "but are unable to get a bearing. Please take a bearing on us and answer by voice on 3105."

She started a steady stream of signals to

help the *Itasca* radiomen locate her plane, but the sound soon drifted and faded.

There wasn't enough time to get a bearing.

The *Itasca* operator tuned to 3105, and for the next forty-five minutes, he called into his microphone every five minutes: "*Itasca* calling. *Itasca* calling."

At 8:45 Amelia Earhart's voice sliced into the radio room. A cold chill entered at the sound of her confused, desperate words: "We are in line of position 157-337 . . . will repeat this message. We will repeat this message at 6120 kilocycles . . . Wait: Listening on 6210 kilocycles. We are running north and south."

The message ended abruptly.

Frantically, the radio operator switched frequencies and went on repeating his message: "*Itasca* calling. *Itasca* calling."

There was no answer. And their half hour of gas was long gone!

Earhart and Noonan were down!

Thompson thought rapidly. The empty fuel tanks might keep the plane afloat for hours. But where?

Where?!!

Amelia Earhart could be anywhere in 400,000 square miles of sea!

Experts said her radio transmitter wouldn't operate while the plane was floating; its aerial would be ineffective. That meant that the only clue to her position was her statement that the plane was in line of position 157-337. That wasn't a radio bearing. It could be a bearing along a sun line. But that was no help! Who knew exactly where along the sun line she was?

Thompson ordered his ship northward out of Howland harbor, sending out messages to Washington, D.C., and San Francisco underway. "Earhart unreported at 0900," he radioed. "Believe down. Am searching probable area and will continue."

The messages stunned Amelia's husband George Putnam in California. The President of the United States and other officials of the U.S. Interior and Navy Departments in Washington, and the San Francisco Division Coast Guard were shaken. The papers picked up the news of Amelia Earhart's disappearance immediately and followed it eagerly; it was "one of the ten most reported news stories of the twentieth century," because millions of people were anxious to learn the outcome of the search for Amelia Earhart.

Official response to Thompson's shocking message in the first days of July, 1937, was instantaneous. The greatest air-sea search for a missing aircraft ever mounted sprang into operation. A seaplane from Hawaii immediately flew to aid the *Itasca* in the first moments of search. The Navy ordered out the enormous battleship *Colorado* and her sister ships, including the carrier *Lexington*. Other smaller craft joined as rapidly as they could get to the area. In all, seven Navy ships and the carrier's planes swept an area of 151,556 square miles of calm seas, in weather that was clear and fine.

But by July 19, when a squadron of seventy-six search planes returned to the deck of the *Lexington* and the search was called off, not one sighting of AE or Noonan had been made. No sign of the wreckage of the Electra had been spotted. Earhart and Noonan and their aircraft had vanished from the face of the earth. America mourned a national hero.

In five years as a pilot, Amelia Earhart had become a legend. In 1932, she flew from Newfoundland to Ireland, the first woman to fly the Atlantic solo. She returned to a ticker-tape parade in New York City, then went on to make other records. In 1935, she crossed the Pacific, and as more and more records fell before her determined onslaught, she became famous. Politicians, scientists, educators, movie personalities, the socially elite — everyone who was anyone — sought her out. She dined with President Franklin D. Roosevelt and took his wife Eleanor up for a nighttime flight.

Soon there was only one unfulfilled dream left — AE wanted to fly around the world. Others had flown shorter routes around the poles; Earhart planned to do it the long way — over the equator.

From Lockheed, she bought the most powerful nonmilitary plane of the day, a 10-E

Electra with twin engines and room for ten passengers. The price was $50,000 before she had the plane stripped and re-equipped to become the "flying laboratory" she laughingly called it. She had larger gas tanks installed to give the plane a 4,500-mile range, as well as a complete navigational room with the latest instruments.

She was thirty-nine years old, and she told a reporter she had a feeling "that there is just about one more good flight left in my system."

That flight began on May 29, 1937. Her flying laboratory winged across the United States, leaving Miami for Puerto Rico; then on to Venezuela, Dutch Guiana, and Brazil. From there her flight plan led across the Atlantic to Senegal. Then she flew across Africa to India and Burma and on to the Dutch East Indies, the island of Timor, Port Darwin in Australia, and finally Lae in New Guinea. Now she faced the last leg of her journey between Hawaii and home.

On July 1, 1937, she and Fred Noonan left Lae. It was the most difficult stretch of her journey, a twenty-hour flight over a lonely and desolate area — 2,556 miles of open water to Howland Island. "I shall be glad," she wrote, "when we have the hazards of its navigation behind us."

But she wasn't worried. Her friend and navigator Fred Noonan had a splendid reputation for knowing the skies over this part of the world. He also had the latest chronometers and compasses and direction finders, and there would be radio signals from ships and shore stations to aid them. For example, the Coast Guard cutter *Itasca* would be stationed near Howland Island for the express purpose of bringing the Electra safely down.

In New Guinea, AE climbed aboard her plane with a smile of confidence, running her hand through her tousled hair. She waved good-bye to the Dutch officials who had come to see her off. With Noonan aboard, she revved the engines to make the heavily laden Electra roll forward, to gain momentum and speed. The airstrip at Lae ended in a cliff overhanging the sea. If she didn't get the plane airborne, AE would plunge down right there. But she cleared just 150 feet from the end of the strip, lifting off for the open skies and seas in the hazardous flight to Howland Island.

Then, eighteen hours later, coming in seriously off course, AE radioed the *Itasca,* speaking in a voice shaken with confusion and quaking with panic. The signal ended abruptly.

It was the last recorded message of a national hero, and the nation *demanded* to know what happened to Amelia Earhart.

There were lots of theories.
One of them said that Earhart and Noonan

landed happily on an uninhabited island where they would share the rest of their lives together.

In mid-July, 1937, the U.S. Navy ended the official search for Amelia Earhart with a terse statement of another theory: "Lost at sea."

Those who agree with this theory think that Amelia Earhart's luck simply ran out. She'd survived three other crashes, but the bad weather and empty spaces over the open Pacific were just too much for her. She crashed in the sea, these people say, and the plane sank, taking her and Noonan down with it. Earhart had taken one risk too many, and she'd paid for it with her life.

Other people think that Amelia Earhart survived *four* crashes, and that there is an untold story about why the Electra went down . . . *and about what* happened to Earhart and Noonan after it crashed!

Basically, this untold story is the same as one in a film released after the Japanese attack on Pearl Harbor that brought the United States into World War II. In a 1943 film called *Flight for Freedom*, starring Rosalind Russell, the actress played a famous and courageous pilot who was very much like Amelia Earhart. In the film, the pilot flew off course *on purpose*.

According to the film, AE hadn't been headed for Howland Island at all when she took off from Lae, New Guinea! She was actually headed into the maze of Japanese-held islands, where she planned to crash-land. The U.S. Navy could then ignore agreements to stay away from the area. They could go in and search for the downed pilot, but could at the same time photograph proof of a build-up of enemy planes and landing ships in the area. The film character learns that the Japanese have discovered the plot and intend to pick her up before the rescue mission can achieve its purpose, so she heroically dives into the ocean near "Gulf," a fortified island held by the Japanese. She is killed, but the U.S. military searches the area anyway; the film character loses her life, but gains the objective of the mission on which she set out.

The film could be dismissed as a good story exept that so much information seems to support it. Earhart's mother, for example, said in 1949, "Amelia told me many things, but there were some things she couldn't tell me. I am convinced she was on some sort of government mission, probably on verbal orders."

Verbal orders. Spies typically are given unwritten orders. That way the government that issued the orders can't be held accountable. No other government can trap them into a war. But the spies — they are on their own.

And later, Earhart's secretary also confirmed the story when she responded positively to the suspicions of an investigative reporter.

The suspicions were these: President Roosevelt recognized in 1937 that a war in the Pacific might not be avoidable. The Japanese were building up huge military encampments on islands in the ocean, and the President wanted to get ready to meet the threat. He wanted to get an arms bill passed by the federal legislature. The American people, however, felt there was no reason to get involved in a war at that time unless it was absolutely necessary. So the President asked Earhart to use her around-the-world flight to either photograph the evidence of Japan's military build-up or to crash on purpose so the U.S. military could search for her and photograph their own evidence. He promised to help support her cover story by providing a hastily built landing strip on Howland Island . . . but his orders were verbal. Unwritten.

The spy theory is supported by natives and Japanese officers who survived the war. They recall seeing Amelia Earhart as a prisoner and say that she was executed on either a Japanese-held island or in Japan itself. Others who support this theory point to wreckage, which may have come from the Electra, that surfaced at a small Japanese-held atoll in the Pacific. If the plane went down there, it would have been an easy matter for a fishing vessel to pick up AE and turn her over to Japanese officials. (Astonishingly, a friend of Amelia's who was also a pilot and had some psychic ability claimed in the first days following her disappearance that the Electra had crashed in the sea close to a Japanese fishing vessel, which was carrying her and Noonan to Japan.)

Whether that is exactly what happened or not, there is no doubt that Commander Thompson of the *Itasca* sensed that something other than an around-the-world flight was going on. Earhart's plane had a radio capable of transmitting 1,000 miles, as well as equally powerful reception capabilities. Yet, even though she obviously knew how to use the equipment, she would not let the Coast Guard cutter know her location. It was as if she didn't *want* them to know where she really was. There were other loose ends, too, misunderstandings that weren't easily explained unless AE had orders Thompson wasn't told about.

She seemed to think, for example, that there was a meteorologist, or weather specialist, aboard the *Itasca,* and there wasn't. In fact, Thompson felt the whole operation had been confused and muddled from the very beginning in mid-June. That's when he had been ordered to take his ship and crew from San Pedro, California, to Howland Island for special duty. In addition to his own San Francisco Division Coast Guard, he was expected to take orders from the Interior and Navy Departments. And to top it off, he'd spent the whole day before Earhart and Noonan took off from New Guinea trying to discover if they'd actually taken off! It was nightfall before he learned they were on their way.

Still, he proceeded on the assumption that AE's plane would arrive sometime after daylight, refuel, and be on its way to Honolulu before returning to the U.S.

So he'd spent the whole night organizing boat parties in case she overshot the island's runway and landed in the surf or farther offshore. He'd ordered groups of men to keep clearing Howland's huge population of dodo birds from the new airstrip, when anyone could see that landing on such a small island with such a lot of birds wasn't practical. He'd stationed a radioman ashore to operate the Navy's experimental new emergency direction finder, ignoring the question that sprang to his mind: Why was new military equipment being tested? He'd gotten searchlights ready to turn on after midnight in case AE picked up a tailwind and arrived early. He'd scheduled the cutter's boilers to make great clouds of smoke at dawn to guide AE in.

Only after that had he waited tensely for AE's first signal. And all the time he'd wondered what was really happening.

What was going on? None of the fuss made sense unless there was more to Amelia Earhart's around-the-world flight than met the eye.

Another variation on the secret spy mission theory of Earhart's disappearance is that she and Noonan were picked up and carried to the island of Saipan, a Japanese stronghold. There, they were tortured until they died. Buried in a grave excavated by CIA operatives when Saipan was conquered, their bones were returned to the United States and are still kept in secret by some agency of the federal government.

Another twist on the Japanese-capture theory is that Earhart was taken to Japan. She lived through interrogation, but was forced to speak on the Tokyo Rose radio show, which sought to demoralize U.S. soldiers in the Pacific Theater during World War II.

The idea that Amelia Earhart survived her fourth crash was the basis for a book in which the authors claimed that she was smuggled into New Jersey to live in secrecy after the war. She was disguised as a nun, but still looked like Earhart, according to the writers. And there was more to support a hidden identity: The nun wore the gold leaf of a major and a Distinguished Flying Cross, an award that only Amelia Earhart was authorized to wear up to that time!

The incognito-nun theory may or may not be true, but many people feel Amelia survived her fourth crash. They claim to have heard from her after she stopped signalling the *Itasca* so abruptly on July 2, 1937.

In the first few days following her disappearance, many ham radio operators reported receiving messages from her. Many of these reports were not followed up because experts claimed that the radio equipment aboard the Electra wouldn't transmit over great distances if the plane were downed.

Other radio messages weren't investigated, either. One of these was picked up on 6210 kilocycles by radiomen on the British-controlled Gilbert Islands *two hours after Amelia supposedly ran out of gas!* A reporter found a U.S. Navy report that states: "At 1030, the morning of the disappearance, Nauru Island radio station picked up Earhart on 6210 kcs saying, 'Land in sight ahead.' "

Another uninvestigated radio message was turned up by the same reporter after six intensive years of research. On July 4, *only days after AE and Noonan supposedly vanished,* three operators at the Navy radio station at Diamond Head, Oahu, Hawaii, heard a voice on wavelength 3105. At first an indistinguishable man's voice was heard. Then on July 7th, a woman's voice was heard saying, "Earhart calling. NRU1 — NRU1 — calling from KHAQQ. On coral southwest of unknown island. Do not know how long we will . . ." The sound faded but a few seconds later, the woman's voice was heard again. "KHAQQ calling. KHAQQ. We are cut a little . . ." The sound faded again and the voice didn't return.

The reporter asked how the Navy man who had given him the report got it.

"One of the operators gave it to me," the man replied. "He felt somebody should know about them."

Were AE and Noonan alive and able to broadcast nearly a week after they supposedly vanished somewhere in the Pacific?

Or was she simply lost at sea while attempting to break yet another record?

Was she on a secret spying mission for the United States, a risk she took knowing that her nation could not officially help her if she failed? If so, did she survive, to be held captive by the enemy and executed when no more information could be gained from her?

Or did she survive enemy interrogation, to be returned to the United States after the war to live a hidden life?

No one knows — officially — but there are intriguing clues that the case has been closed secretly. For example, her husband was able to convince a court that Amelia Earhart was legally dead only eighteen months after she disappeared, a process that usually takes seven years. What evidence did he present in court to gain that ruling that quickly?

And why are government records about

her disappearance still withheld so stubbornly?

Before Amelia Earhart left on the flight that would be her last, she wrote a letter to her husband. He read it aloud for reporters after the search was stopped. "Please know," she wrote, "I am quite aware of the hazzards. I want to do it — because I want to do it. Women must try to do things as men have tried. When they fail, their failure must be but a challenge to others." AE had also told him once that "I'd like to go in my plane. Quickly."

Did she?

Officially, no one knows.

Thomas Riha

When Professor Thomas Riha didn't show up to teach his classes in Russian history at the University of Colorado in Boulder on March 18, 1969, no one worried too much about it. In fact, his nephew didn't even bother to tell the Missing Persons Bureau that his uncle had vanished until October — almost seven months later!

When police talked to Dr. Joseph Smiley, the president of the university, he shrugged off the suggestion that the matter was serious. He said he had information from "reliable sources" in Washington, D.C., that led him to believe that Riha was "alive and well."

"What do you mean?" investigators asked him, but Smiley wouldn't answer.

"I've been sworn to secrecy," he said, and although he felt a "real regret" that he couldn't explain further, police and reporters had to understand that "a confidence is still a confidence."

A university colleague of Professor Riha's talked to the Denver office of the Immigration and Naturalization Service, because the professor had been born in Czechoslovakia and was a naturalized citizen of the United States. People in the office told the man not to worry; Riha was definitely alive. Several months later, the man checked again. This time, a cautious voice told him mysteriously that it was probably "better not to be interested in the Riha matter."

A reporter talked to Gloria Forest McPherson Scimo Tannenbaum, a friend of Riha's who went by the name of Galya Tannenbaum, in Colorado. She had followed the professor there from Illinois, where she had served time in a penitentiary after being convicted of forgery and embezzlement charges in 1959. Don't worry, Mrs. Tannenbaum told the reporter, Riha is all right. He's somewhere between Montreal and Toronto in a "summer-resort sort of place," she said. He left, she added blithely, to escape his troublesome young wife.

Authorities talked with Hana, who had been Riha's wife for only five months before he disappeared. She didn't have much to tell them. In fact, one night about a week before her husband disappeared, she caused a stir in the neighborhood when she ran screaming from their home. Neighbors said that she smelled overpoweringly of ether and that she was extremely upset. Terrified, they said. Immediately after that night, Mrs. Riha left Colorado to stay with friends in New York City.

Riha disappeared completely from his usual life, but family, friends, and agencies of the federal government were quick to assure police, reporters, and fellow faculty members that Riha was fine. He's just fine, they said, don't worry. Don't concern yourself.

But investigators *were* concerned. Riha may have been alive and well and living somewhere in Canada in a "summer-resort sort of place," but why was everyone being so mysterious about it? They were acting as if his disappearance was top secret! Then, too, events following his disappearance were strange and unexplainable. And on top of that, the search for the missing man was being blocked actively by agencies of the federal government that included the FBI, the CIA, and the State Department!

What *had* happened to Professor Thomas Riha? What was behind all the attempts to stop the search for him, to cover up his disappearance? Exactly who — and what — was he?

On the surface Riha, a highly intelligent man, was just another immigrant to the United States. After he came to this country in 1947, he took his Bachelor's and Master's degrees at the University of California at Berkeley, and got his Ph.D. at Harvard in 1962. In 1964 he published a three-volume study, *Readings in Russian Civilization*. He taught Russian history at the University of Chicago and at Marburg University in West Germany before he came to the University of Colorado. There, he collected religious statues and bought books, and when the Russians invaded Czechoslovakia in 1968, he helped his nephew, Zednek Cerveny, to escape that country and find a home near him. Toward the end of that year, he married twenty-five-year old Hana Hruskova, who had also been born in Czechoslovakia. Then, only a few months later, she fled their four-bedroom house in terror.

And a week after that, Riha vanished.

He left a house full of furniture, his collection of statues, a 1,000-book library, his car, and — oddest of all — a kitchen table that was set for breakfast.

If that wasn't strange enough, a series of odd events began then, although authorities didn't learn about all of them right away.

One of the first unusual events happened a few weeks after the professor vanished. His friend Galya called his nephew Zednek Cerveny. She told him matter-of-factly that Riha would never return and that it was necessary for the two of them to have a serious talk. They met, and Galya handed Cerveny two pistols with a flourish, telling him she was a brigadier general in military intelligence. *She* had helped him escape the Russian invasion of his homeland, she said, and now the professor had asked her to help again. He wanted her to take charge of disposing of his personal effects. She said she'd told him she would, and she began immediately.

Galya quickly arranged to sell Riha's car to a Denver public school official; the signature on the auto's title assignment appeared to be Riha's. She moved all Riha's furniture and personal papers to her own home in Denver and sold his house. She donated his art collection, valued at around $19,000, to the Denver Art Museum. She gave his books to Loretto Heights College in Denver. Royalty checks from Riha's three-volume book suddenly started to appear at Mrs. Tannenbaum's home.

Letters, supposedly from Riha, that supported all these arrangements came to his lawyer's office. The attorney wasn't impressed by these; the handwriting was different from Riha's and the letters were full of grammatical errors Riha wouldn't have made. Mrs. Tannenbaum wasn't intimidated by the lawyer's doubts; she calmly went on disposing of Riha's belongings.

She finished this, only to find herself swamped with other crises and sadnesses. Her friends were dying. They were swallowing doses of cyanide poisons and dropping like flies. Gustav F. Ingwerson, a Denver painter, inventor, and plastics designer, died on June 16, 1969. Potassium-cyanide poisoning. Oddly, Professor Riha's engraved wedding ring was found among Ingwerson's personal effects. Equally strange, Ingwerson's will seemed to be witnessed by Riha's nephew, although Cerveny later denied witnessing the document in a Denver Probate Court. Curiously, Ingwerson's will granted items including a color TV, a cuckoo clock, and a dinosaur bone to Mrs. Tannenbaum, as well as making the more expected bequests to his own family.

Three months later, another of Galya's close friends was found dead. Mrs. Barbara Elbert died in her Denver apartment on September 13, 1969. Sodium-cyanide poisoning.

Denver police suspected that Mrs. Tannenbaum was directly involved in both of these cases, as well as in the Riha disappearance, but they couldn't find the evidence to charge her. Instead, remembering her earlier conviction for forgery, they took another look at the signature on Ingwerson's will and the letters to Riha's lawyer and nodded. They waited for Galya to go one signature too far.

It wasn't long before she did. She chartered a plane for Cerveny from a Colorado flying service, telling the pilot that she was a Secret Service agent and that the plane was being hired for two citizens of the Soviet Union.

She offered a check signed by Riha in payment. The check was bad and the signature, suspicious. At last, police were able to charge Galya with something. She was brought to trial for forgery.

Boulder District Court proceedings against Mrs. Tannenbaum went quickly. Galya immediately pleaded not guilty by reason of insanity; the court didn't hesitate to find her legally insane. The judge rapped a gavel and ordered her confined at the Colorado State Hospital in Pueblo.

Early in March, 1971, Galya started to dispose of more possessions, this time her own. She gave away her things to other inmates, and then sat down and wrote a farewell letter to her lawyer: "I didn't do Tom or Gus or Barb in. . . . Everything that has made me feel good about myself has been taken away. Life is very cheap." She stretched out on her bed, reached for a small pill, and swallowed it. Cyanide.

No one knows where or how she got the poison pill, but hospital authorities heard her last words. "I didn't kill him," she said, speaking of Riha. "He's in Russia! He just made it!"

Her suicide slammed the door on that avenue of the Riha investigation, but police and reporters went doggedly on. They combed the mountains around Boulder, hiking the roads and crawling down abandoned mine shafts. They found nothing.

One reporter dug up the entire earth basement in Mrs. Tannenbaum's Denver home, thinking that she might have murdered the professor and buried him there. It was possible, the reporter thought, because even if nothing had been found to link her officially with the Ingwerson and Elbert deaths, Galya had certainly been involved with them in one way or another. Also, she had been in the Riha home the night Hana bolted away, quaking with terror and reeking of ether. Violent and unpredictable things happened whenever Galya Tannenbaum was around, so digging up her basement for the body of the missing man was worth a try. But that attempt, like all the others, didn't unearth a single clue to the whereabouts of Professor Thomas Riha.

Where was he? What had happened to him? Efforts to find the answers to those questions were being shunted into still more blind avenues by powerful forces.

Mysterious "reliable sources" in the federal government kept insisting that Riha was alive and well. The FBI, the CIA, and the State Department denied that they took any part in Riha's disappearance, but proof that they did cropped up later in court records. One such document, for example, states that an FBI agent stationed in Denver frantically told a CIA agent to "calm this thing down. . . . Get out to the press that Riha is alive and well."

When J. Edgar Hoover, then head of the FBI, heard about this, he demanded that the CIA tell him the name of the agent. The CIA said they wouldn't. That's where matters stood for several years, with the two intelligence agencies stoutly refusing to give out any information about their involvement with the Riha case. And if they wouldn't talk to each other, they certainly wouldn't talk to the police or the newspapers! The police investigation was effectively shut down, but the *Denver Post* was more insistent about getting some answers.

In 1975, at the newspaper's request, U.S. Senator Gary Hart of Colorado brought up the Riha case once again. Hart asked questions about the fate of Professor Thomas Riha during the Senate Select Committee on Intelligence Activities, and this time the questions were answered. The CIA's former chief of counterintelligence James A. Angleton, and the former director of the FBI's intelligence division Charles Brennan were on the spot. They talked.

Who had told university president Joseph Smiley that Riha was alive and well?

"We did," the CIA's Angleton admitted.

Other representatives of the CIA added more information. When Riha was an exchange student in Moscow in 1958, the agency had thought of using the professor as a spy, but they'd reconsidered and decided not to. Not only was Riha not a spy for us, the representatives went on, there was also "no information to suggest that Riha was a Soviet agent, or for that matter, a double agent."

What about Galya Tannenbaum — was she an agent?

No! said the CIA, giving the same answer they had given earlier about their involvement with Riha.

No! said the FBI, giving the same answer they had given earlier about their involvement with Riha.

And what happened to Professor Thomas Riha?

The CIA submitted a memo that spoke of a "possible sighting" of the missing man in Czechoslovakia in 1973.

The FBI didn't have any idea what could have or had happened to Thomas Riha.

The information from the CIA and the FBI raised more questions than it answered. Was Riha a spy? Was he a double agent? Had he been forced to leave his breakfast one morning in March and drop suddenly out of sight in order to escape behind the Iron Curtain?

According to her dying words, Galya Tannenbaum thought this was the case. Riha was a spy and he was now safely in Russia.

Riha's nephew Cerveny told a reporter that his uncle's body was probably somewhere in the mountains, but he didn't mention why he thought so. He didn't use the word *spy*, either.

Senator Hart summed up his conclusions for the newspaper: "Riha is, most probably, living in Czechoslovakia. . . . Why he left the U.S. remains unclear."

If nagging questions about Thomas Riha remain, so do some about Galya Tannenbaum.

Who were the two Soviet citizens for whom she attempted to charter a plane? She used Cerveny's name, but she had used his name before to witness an allegedly fraudulent will. Had Riha, after hiding himself carefully and successfully somewhere on the North American continent, sent Galya to charter the plane that would carry the two of them to Russia? Or was Galya simply insane? Was she only playing out the role of spy that she created in her unbalanced mind, right down to the taking of the poison pellet that is issued to spies for use as a last resort?

Her last words were peculiar. "He's in Russia!" she said. "He just made it!" She spoke as if some definite timeline had just been fulfilled. As if she'd been in touch with Riha recently and knew his exact schedule. Perhaps her words meant nothing and were only a figment of her imagination — a delusion. But if that's true, a chilling new question arises.

Where, after being searched and held under close observation, did she get the cyanide pill?

No one knows any more about *that* than they do about Professor Thomas Riha's true fate.

Alice Van Alstine

March 26, 1976, was Friday night, the end of a week. It was also the end of Alice Van Alstine's time to live in her Des Moines apartment.

She left in a hurry, going into the wintery Iowa night without her shoes. She also left her coat, her children, her purse, and her money behind. And, chillingly, the key was still in the ignition of her abandoned car when investigators arrived. The car door hung open.

Investigators think she went without a struggle, maybe even willingly. There were no signs of unusual disorder, except for the strangely deserted car and one broken bottle on the floor of the apartment. The car has never been explained, but maybe Alice's sister-in-law shed some light on the smashed bottle when she said that Alice was an "atrocious housekeeper." The bottle could be an important clue, but it could also mean absolutely nothing.

In fact, even if investigators had found the walls full of bullet holes, *that* could have meant nothing. Alice's sister said that when she had visited Alice in another house, the walls there were pockmarked with bullet holes, for which there was a reasonable explanation. Alice and her first husband, Lee Andre, had simply used walls and doors and piles of old magazines to absorb slugs when they practiced indoor target shooting. Alice, her sister added, was an excellent shot — the first woman to make a club rifle team at Iowa State University.

Wherever Alice Van Alstine was going when she left her apartment so mysteriously and abruptly that Friday night in late March, she went forever. She disappeared thoroughly and completely; no one has seen her since.

The Polk County Sheriff's Department questioned over 200 people in their attempt to discover what happened to her. They called deputies from other counties to help in the search, too, one group of them scouring 240 acres around a large, half-finished house in the rolling countryside of southern Iowa. The Andres had once begun to build there. Deputies found no trace of Alice, but they uncovered something else that alarmed them — an illegal machine gun, carefully wrapped in a waterproof casing.

That discovery brought the Iowa Bureau of Criminal Investigation into the search. Federal agents from the U.S. Treasury Department's Alcohol, Tobacco and Firearms office also got involved, both because of the machine gun and because of the books Alice left behind when she vanished.

Alice Van Alstine had a curious library. It contained books on brainwashing, riots, and revolution; racist religious books; catalogs and manuals about machine guns and explosives; literature and stickers produced by an organization called the Minutemen.

Alice had once belonged to the group, a paramilitary organization whose members believe that Communists plan to take over our government. They believe this so firmly that they consider anyone who believes in and works for peace to be an enemy, a traitor. Minutemen secretly stockpile illegal weapons, explosives, food, and medicines to prepare for the national emergency that will follow the downfall of our nation.

Alice hadn't talked a lot about her association with the Minutemen; a family member said she seemed to be "afraid to say anything" about the group's activities. But a Minuteman symbol had hung on the door of Alice and Lee Andre's home, and occasionally she had spoken of a gang of men who practiced war maneuvers at night in four-wheel-drive vehicles equipped with CB radios.

Sometimes she tried to convince people that these war games were just that — "all a big game." She laughed about one "game" that involved an old car of hers, which Minutemen spray-painted black so they could drive it undetected at night. One of the men got so carried away that he sprayed the windshield and side windows, only to find he had to scrape them clean in order to drive at all!

Most Minutemen hide the fact of their membership more carefully than Alice did. Robert DePugh of Missouri, who founded the group in 1959 and watched it grow to be active throughout the nation by the mid-1960s, told a reporter that no member is "authorized" to say he or she is a member: "If a suspected Minuteman says, 'Yes, I'm a member,' then you can assume he's not."

He also denied that members of his organization stockpile weapons, but authorities have arrested people known to be Minutemen and seized large caches of arms and explosives all over the country — in Los Angeles, in large cities in New York and Connecticut, and in the Midwest. One Minutemen cache included three machine guns, six cases of dynamite, 800 detonating caps, a plunger-type detonator, and 200 rounds of ammunition. It was discovered in a locked hangar at a small airport in Iowa in 1969, but no one was charged with illegal possession of the machine guns — because no one *could* be. There were 40 sets of keys to the hangar, and officials couldn't be sure who owned what!

DePugh doesn't deny the beliefs of his underground organization, nor does he deny that its activities are shrouded in secrecy. He's proud of his firm control of the Minutemen. In April, 1973, when he was paroled from a federal prison in Atlanta, Georgia, where he had been serving a sentence both for illegal possession of firearms and for jumping bail and failing to appear in court, he said the Minutemen had been inactive during his imprisonment. By 1975, when a building of the American Friends Service Committee (Quakers) in Des Moines was shattered by a bomb, DePugh was free and the Minutemen were back in action. The bombing is still officially unsolved, but Alice clipped and saved newspaper reports of it, telling her sister that the Minutemen bombed the building as a warning to the Quakers to stop their "traitorous" peace efforts.

Alice and Lee Andre shared political ideas, and they both loved their four children. Alice worried about how they would survive the aftermath of the Communist takeover. She worried about the survival of the rest of her family, too. In 1970 she sent her father a letter in which she said that all the signs pointed to the speedy arrival of the Revolution. It might come this summer or next, she wrote, but it was inevitable. She wrote that past members of the Communist Party had gone on record with the announcement that the world takeover goal was set for 1976, and that the Communists were ahead of schedule.

There would be a final war between "God's Liberty and Satan's Communism." Alice wanted her father to take the two- or three-day hike between their homes to be with the Andres if conditions grew bad where he was. She asked him to bring with him all the food, clothes, and ammunition he had. The Andres had weapons.

"Interchangeable ammunition is 30.06, .22 cal., 12 gauge, 9mm, .45 cal.," she wrote, knowing that her father would understand these instructions because he had been a small arms sergeant in World War II. She asked him to bring extra weapons of these caliber if he could because they would also be arranging for extra ammunition.

Several years later, the Andres began building the large house in southern Iowa. The place was on a steep hill, hidden in 240 acres of thick woods, and it was nearly inaccessible. It was a fortress.

Before it was finished, the Andres' marriage began to break up and they separated. Alice took some of the couple's stockpiled arms and stored them in her father's barn: 6,000 rounds of .30-caliber ammunition, a half case of red phosphorous tracer ammunition for night shooting, and a half case of .45-caliber ammunition. She showed her father a U.S. Army booby trap she had kept in her kitchen cabinet.

When she filed for divorce, she gave a deposition under oath to an attorney as part of the proceedings. She said that suitcases belonging to Minutemen were left at her home when she was married to Andre. One of the suitcases contained a Bible with coded messages, but all of the suitcases had been burned to keep their secrets from authorities. Stolen weapons and explosives were stored in her barn, she said, adding that the explosives had been used to bomb a Des Moines building. She said she had been visited by FBI agents. She talked about building the fortresslike country home.

Alice was talking openly of Minutemen business now, and she was no longer trying to convince anyone that the whole thing was a game. Several days after she gave the deposition, relatives learned that the Minutemen's reaction to it was swift and terrifying. Three men wearing Halloween masks came in the night and kidnapped her. They warned her to stop talking, and they threatened to kill her if she didn't.

Alice didn't report the kidnapping because

she was frightened. She thought she recognized the voice of one of the kidnappers, and if he was who she thought he was, he had influence with the police. "Dad," she told her father, "they are going to kill me."

She began taking flying lessons, calling her instructor one day to tell him that if she didn't see him in the next three or four days, she wanted him to call her father. She said a gang was after her.

Alice's divorce was granted on January 3, 1975, and she married Merlyn Everett Van Alstine the same day. She divorced him on January 1, 1976; on March 26, 1976, Alice Van Alstine vanished.

A week later, an undated letter signed "A.A." arrived at the home of a friend of Andre's in Utah. Police dismissed the letter as a fake.

What happened to Alice Van Alstine?

Was there really a "gang" after her, as she told her flying instructor?

If so, could the mysterious gang have been a group of Minutemen making good on their threat to kill her, as she reported to members of her family?

Or had she escaped them or another, unknown threat by running barefooted into the wintry March night and a secure hiding place?

Former husband Lee Andre has a theory

of what happened to Alice Van Alstine. He thinks she saved money and became what he called an "adult dropout."

Descriptions of Alice's personality lend some support to that theory. Her sister noted how deeply Alice became involved in whatever she was doing. She seemed to sponge up the personalities of other people and become like them. If the people around her in March, 1976, had talked about dropping out and finding a new life, Alice may have done it.

One of Alice's friends mentioned another facet of her personality that could fit in with the "dropout" theory. Alice was intelligent and sensitive, but she also loved intrigue and mystery. When she confided to her flying instructor that a gang was after her, she had added that she was a member of the American Nazi Party. Dropping out and disappearing — especially after delivering murky hints like this — could be very satisfying to someone who loved intrigue and mystery.

But most relatives and friends think Alice wouldn't leave without her children. They recalled how much Alice loved her raccoon and other pets when she was a child; they pointed out that she loved her children in the same strongly protective way now that she was thirty years old. "She might run off, but she'd always take the kids with her. . . . Alice was a real dingbat of a mother . . . but she loved her kids," her former sister-in-law told a reporter.

Still, when police came to Alice's apartment the night she disappeared, they found three young children left alone.

Police did what they could in a situation in which there was no evidence of foul play. They swore out a warrant. Alice was wanted for child desertion.

Alice never appeared to face the charge.

Why did Alice Van Alstine snatch up her car keys and run from her apartment barefooted? Was she fleeing some threat that followed her relentlessly, pulled her from her car, and put an end to any hope of escape?

The detective sergeant in the Polk County Sheriff's Department who was in charge of the investigation thinks that's what happened to Alice Van Alstine. He feels she was kidnapped, then murdered. But his investigation could find no reason for anyone to do that, and he doesn't think the Minutemen had anything to do with it. He knows that Alice had been involved with them, but says that that was too long before she disappeared for there to be a logical connection. There would be no good reason for them to follow through on their old murder threat.

Relatives and friends think Alice was kidnapped and murdered, too. "Her body's on the bottom of the Saylorville Reservoir," one of them said, but wouldn't mention who she thought put it there. Other friends and family members aren't so reluctant to name the people they suspect. "She knew too much about Minutemen activities in Iowa," one said. "She wanted nothing more to do with them, so they considered her a traitor."

Howard Barnes, Alice's father, agrees. When she told him before she disappeared that the Minutemen were going to kill her, he said he "couldn't comprehend" it. "I couldn't picture that they were that vicious a bunch," he told a reporter.

But when Alice vanished, Barnes mounted his own investigation. He spent a year driving thousands of miles to talk to people about his daughter's connections with the Minutemen, and he no longer has doubts. Because of what he learned, he feels as threatened as Alice had. He no longer sleeps soundly in his bed. Now, he sleeps warily and lightly on his couch, with a loaded .30-caliber carbine within easy reach. The gun is protection against the Minutemen, whom he firmly believes murdered his daughter.

There is, however, no gun that can protect him against the other thing he fears — that his own house will be bombed with explosives taken from secret, hidden stockpiles.

Was Alice Van Alstine really murdered? No one knows.

Michael Rockefeller

The storm sprang up offshore about eleven miles from the primitive village of Agats, when they were roughly halfway there. The catamaran started shipping water in the rolling seas, and the four men in the boat bailed frantically. It didn't help; the flimsy craft capsized in the angry Aragura Sea between the southern coast of New Guinea and Australia.

The two native guides on board swam for shore to get help. The two white men stayed with the boat, clinging to it all night. Early the next morning, they took stock of their situation. Already they had drifted about three miles from shore. What should they do?

One of the men, thirty-four-year-old Rene Wassing, thought they should stay with the boat. The tide was against them, pulling them out to open sea now. Swimming for shore would be difficult and energy-consuming. They would be better off hanging on until rescue came. Wassing was hopeful someone would find them; the Dutch government of New Guinea patrolled the waters. And even if the Dutch patrol boats didn't happen upon them, Wassing was sure that when they didn't keep to their expedition schedule a search for them would be mounted. Whether it was a sea hunt or an aerial search, the wreckage of the boat would be far easier to spot than the two of them would be in the dense mangrove and *loraro* swamps ashore.

The other man, twenty-three-year-old Michael Rockefeller, didn't agree. He was impatient, and he thought there wasn't any point in wasting time drifting around and waiting to be rescued. The two natives obviously hadn't been able to find help, so he wanted to swim for shore and see what he could do. He was sure he could reach land; he was big — 6′ 1″ — and in good shape.

"I think I can make it," he said.

Wassing thought Rockefeller probably could make a three-mile swim, but this was no ordinary three miles. He warned Rockefeller about the shark-infested waters and the hungry crocodiles that swarmed on the shore. "I can take no responsibility for you," he said.

Rockefeller responded by tying a red jerrican and the outboard's gas tank together for buoyancy; he'd use those to help keep himself afloat. Then he stripped to his shorts, grabbed his improvised "life jacket," and set out, paddling confidently toward the menacing shore.

Wassing watched: "I followed him until I could only see three dots — his head and the two red cans. Then he disappeared across my horizon."

Wassing was rescued eight hours later by a Dutch patrol boat. He had drifted twenty-two miles from shore. Several days later, a floating gas tank was spotted 120 miles down the coast, but Michael Rockefeller was no longer using it for buoyancy. He had vanished.

Officials ordered a search for Rockefeller and notified his family. Only days after he disappeared, Rockefeller's father, the Governor of New York, spent $38,000 to charter a jet and join the hunt, saying he "could never forgive" himself if he "didn't do everything possible to help find" his son. Michael's twin sister Mary Strawbridge went to New Guinea with her father. Once there, they flew over the southern coastline in a two-engine Dakota, spelling each other with field glasses as they anxiously sought a trace of Michael in the swampy jungle below.

They weren't the only ones searching for the missing man. The Rockefellers offered 250 sticks of tobacco to any native who would look for the missing Rockefeller. That was great wealth to the natives, and thousands of them turned out to help, shoving off into the swamps in their canoes or hacking their way on foot through the dense jungle plants along the coast. The government of New Guinea assigned boats and airplanes and marines to the search. The Australians dispatched helicopters. When President John F. Kennedy telegraphed sympathy and offered to help, the U.S. Seventh Fleet volunteered a carrier and planes.

The Rockefellers soon left the search to all these fresh, expert eyes and set up headquarters at the district commissioner's house in Merauke, anxiously waiting for news that was never to come. No trace of Michael Rockefeller ever surfaced after Wassing saw his bobbing head disappear from the horizon.

It's a long way from New York to New Guinea, but Michael Rockefeller had made the trip twice. In 1960, the year before he disappeared, he graduated from Harvard. He wanted to do something exciting before he settled down to a staid career in finance. After serving six months in the U.S. Army, he signed on as sound technician for an expedition sponsored by Harvard's Peabody Museum. He would help film and record the customs of primitive tribes in the dark-green wilderness that is the interior of New Guinea. No one knew much about how the natives lived and thought other than that they had been headhunters in the past. Headhunting — killing someone from another tribe, then severing, shrinking, and painting the head —

had been outlawed by the government of the island. But it takes more than a law to change the way a people has lived for as long as they can remember, so there was an element of danger in the trip.

"Why do you want to go there?" a reporter asked Rockefeller.

"It's the desire to do something romantic and exciting," he answered, "at a time when frontiers in the real sense of the word are disappearing."

Rockefeller saw it as an adventure, and he had a good time in the rugged freedom of the jungle. He grew a beard on the demanding hike inland, became Indian-wrestling champion of the expedition, and enjoyed his work. He was fascinated with the Papuan natives' war chants and their singing that sounded like tooth-grinding.

When the Harvard expedition ended in September, 1961, Rockefeller came home and spent some time with his parents, but he still wasn't ready to settle down into a three-piece-suit career. He had become entranced with the wood carvings done by the Asmat tribe who lived along the southern shore of New Guinea. All the time he was home, Michael was planning to return to New Guinea on a three-month-long expedition of his own, to collect shields, painted skulls, and twenty-foot-long *mbis* poles for the museum of primitive art founded by his father.

This time he would travel with only one

other white men, Rene Wassing. Wassing was an ethnologist, a scientist who compares and analyzes cultures. Rockefeller would be an "assistant ethnologist." The two would get native help when they needed it on their journey among the Asmats.

Soon the plans were complete, and Rockefeller left to carry them out. He and Wassing went to village after village, trading shells and axes for more than fifty pieces of art. In some of the villages along the swampy coast, the two stayed at missions of the Crozier Fathers, where Rockefeller showed off his boat. It was a thirty-foot *proa,* a catamaran made of two native dugout canoes lashed together by planks, powered by an 18-h.p. outboard motor.

The priests weren't as impressed with the boat as Rockefeller was; they cautioned him that the coastal tides swelled twenty feet high and surged seventy-five miles upriver before they swept out again. The powerful tides challenged even the best native rowers, who knew how to handle them. The priests warned Rockefeller that his boat wasn't safe. Rockefeller scoffed at them as he did at Wassing on that December morning in 1961 when he struck out for shore and swam into the unknown.

What happened to Michael Rockefeller? Did he drown? Was he devoured by sharks or crocodiles?

Is there any truth in filmmaker Lorne Blai's dreadful theory about his fate? In 1977 Blair went to New Guinea to record the art of the Asmat tribe, and he claimed to have learned that Rockefeller *did* survive the dangerous swim to shore. He said that Asmat tribesmen fell on Rockefeller as he staggered to land. They killed him and hacked up his body, which was then eaten by a subchief named Ari. Blair asked Ari point-blank if this is what happened to Rockefeller and the man responded by laughing. Blair, knowing that the natives of that area were said to practice cannibalism, took the man's laugh to be an admission that Rockefeller had been cannibalized.

Assuming you know what someone from a different culture means by a laugh is dangerous, however. Even a simple gesture like nodding your head doesn't mean yes all over the world. Ari's laugh could have meant anything. It could have been only an amazed reaction to a silly question. After all, headhunting and cannibalism were against the law.

Was Michael Rockefeller eaten by a cannibal? No one knows. But it *is* known that expeditions to New Guinea had led to trouble in the past.

On the first expedition to the interior, the leader of the Harvard group had made missionaries and Dutch district officers angry. The U.S. scientists, they said, were stirring the headhunters into tribal warfare so they could film the battles! The judicial branch of the United Nations, The Hague, sent a parliamentary commission to investigate, and their report supported the complaints. "It was known to the authorities," the report read, "that the leader of the expedition was very keen on filming tribal warfare. In the first two months after the arrival of the expedition, there were about seven deaths and a dozen or more wounded in and around a village called Kurulu."

And New Guinea officials weren't any happier with the way Rockefeller's second, smaller expedition to the coast was going. One official said, "Michael's presence led to a tremendous increase in local trade, especially in beautifully painted human heads. A few weeks ago members of the head-hunter tribe approached the area administrator for permission to go head-hunting 'for one evening only, please, sir.' This was because Michael was offering ten steel hatchets for one head. We had to warn him off, as he was creating a demand that could not be met without bloodshed."

Rockefeller's enthusiasm was understandable. He was collecting artifacts in an area that is still relatively fresh ground for scholars — Oceania, a great series of South Sea Islands that includes New Guinea. The rare and valuable objects he brought back could make his reputation, and would certainly add immeasurably to the museum's holdings. Without collectors like Rockefeller, the art of Oceania is soon lost, destroyed by the heat and humidity of the area. For example, *mbis* poles, the tall totemlike poles of male figures stacked head to toe, are made from wood, and they disintegrate in a relatively short length of time. In New Guinea, the poles are installed at 45-degree angles outside Asmat ceremonial houses to serve two purposes: to memorialize the victims of head-hunting raids and to remind the living that the deaths must be avenged. Today nine *mbis* poles, sent by Michael Rockefeller before he disappeared, hold a central place in the Oceanic section of the Rockefeller wing of the Metropolitan Museum of Art.

They may be the best possible memorial for Michael Rockefeller, because he, too, was a headhunter. He hunted for a museum, but that's a fine distinction in the long view. He may have paid the same harsh, primitive price for his trophies as the New Guinea natives did for theirs. In the deep jungles of New Guinea, Michael Rockefeller was lost . . . and never found.

Dr. Charles Brancati

On November 19, 1928, Dr. Charles Brancati scrambled from his car, shouted some of the weirdest last words ever recorded, and scuttled into New York City's Pelham Parkway subway station.

He was never seen again, although police searched diligently for him for three years in an endeavor that led them into strange blind alleys. They would undertake a search for a second missing person — the mysterious, shadowy figure of a man named Luigi Romano. They would find themselves unexpectedly thrust into the company of some of the most notorious and hardened gangsters of the mob-ridden 1920s.

Police approached the case seriously, of course, but the circumstances surrounding Brancati's disappearance are so bizarre and the personalities involved so flamboyant that it's impossible not to see dark humor in what happened — especially since Brancati's last recorded words were so *odd*.

What were they?

"Paint the place," Brancati shouted just before he disappeared. "The whole house!"

These are hardly the words of a man who isn't planning to come back, and George Rheinish certainly didn't think they were.

Rheinish was Brancati's handyman; it was to him that Brancati shouted. It was just one more surprise for Rheinish that Sunday morning. Earlier, Brancati had startled Rheinish by summoning him from the cottage he shared with his wife Daisy to the estate's mansion.

"Drive me to the subway," Brancati ordered. "I have to get to the office."

On a Sunday? But the doctor's office was at 411 East 116th Street; surely the doctor didn't need to go all the way from the Bronx to Manhattan today!

"It's urgent!" Brancati insisted. "I have to get to my office without delay!"

Well, an order was an order.

Rheinish shrugged and drove his employer to the subway station, wondering why the doctor was so nervous. He was sweating and twitching and obviously anxious to avoid wasting time.

Why? Rheinish wondered. What was the trouble? And why, the second the doctor left the car, did he stop to shout this new shocker?

Paint the place? The whole house? That would take some doing!

Dr. Brancati lived in the old Gouverneur Morris mansion overlooking Long Island Sound.

And what color should he paint the place? Rheinish asked himself. Brancati lived alone. He'd never married, so there was no wife to ask.

Well, an order was an order. . . .

As he drove back to the mansion through the sparse Sunday morning traffic, Rheinish decided he would paint the place according to what he knew of the doctor's taste. Brancati liked things bright and ornate. He liked the grand manner. Lots of colors and lots of curlicues, Rheinish thought, that's what the doctor will want.

That's exactly what Rheinish gave him, but Brancati never returned to approve the work.

Not that he vanished from the face of the earth without another trace. Brancati sent letters.

Not notes to friends; Brancati didn't have many. His main contacts were the brokers who handled his investments and the patients he saw in his busy medical practice. Brancati's correspondence was confined to his brothers Oreste, Edward, and Ernesto.

At first his letters bore postmarks from Passaic, New Jersey, close to home; then they were mailed from farther away — first from Canada, finally from London. Then, after four months, he stopped writing altogether. Finally his brother decided to go to the police and report him missing.

By the time the police came to inspect the old Morris mansion, the crisp, new edge had gone from Rheinish's astonishing paint job, but it was still garish and vibrant enough to be breathtaking. Police found the place unexpected in another way, too.

It was, frankly, a mess. There was dust and dirt everywhere. Scraps of paper littered the floors. Pieces of furniture were knocked around helter-skelter. It appeared that the house had been thoroughly — and violently — searched.

Police looked in Brancati's upstairs bedroom and found still more to surprise them. There was a litter of torn paper on the floor here, too, but there was also a heap of the oddest debris ever encountered by any of the officers on the scene. They made a list of the evidence for their report:

- Three dozen bottles of ginger ale
- One pair of women's slippers
- One manicure set
- Various keen-edged surgical instruments
- Several discarded medical books

And, more alarmingly, they noted a wall riddled with bullet holes, a spent slug on the mantelpiece, and a threatening letter on a chair.

Someone had taken the time and trouble to write, but neglected to sign or date his letter. "You Big Villain," it began, and then the writer scribbled his way through some obscenities and profanities before setting down to serious business. It appeared that the writer had a problem; a woman had jilted him. He was extremely upset — actually, violently furious. The writer advised that the best solution to this problem would be for the "Big Villain" — presumably Brancati — to put her out. If he didn't, the writer concluded vigorously, "I'll cut your throat like a sheep's."

Police glanced around. Brancati's house was obviously the victim of someone menacing, and so, probably, was Brancati. After all, his brothers said he was missing.

But after police found other evidence in Brancati's bedroom, they wondered if he *was* gone. Neatly folded in a chair near the middle of the room were freshly pressed trousers — eight pairs of them! It was possible that someone was borrowing Brancati's pants, of course, but it was also possible that Brancati was still around!

Perhaps he had simply doubled back on the false trail he had laid with the letters to his brothers. Perhaps he was only hiding out in a place where no one would think of looking for him — his own home.

Then police discovered that close to a quarter of a million dollars had been withdrawn from one of the doctor's brokerage accounts. Perhaps, they thought for the first time, Brancati had been kidnapped for ransom.

Kidnap was a reasonable explanation of the doctor's disappearance, because further investigation revealed that he had a personal worth of around one million dollars. Dr. Brancati was a wealthy man, although he hadn't always been so.

As a young man, Brancati immigrated from Naples, Italy, with his three brothers, and washed dishes to work his way through the Columbia College of Physicians and Surgeons. When he graduated, he opened what became a successful practice in the densely populated Italian community on Manhattan's east side, and grew slowly and steadily rich. By the time he disappeared, Brancati's wealth included apartment buildings and large holdings of stocks and bonds.

Now one fourth of that wealth had been transferred to a mysterious man named Luigi Romano! When police asked who had ordered the transfer, they discovered that Brancati himself had done so by letter. And, surprisingly, the letter had been sent in the first few days following the man's disappearance!

Investigators followed up. Executives at the brokerage house recalled why they hadn't questioned the transfer of such a huge sum — they had merely been following Brancati's wishes, they said. Weeks before he disappeared, the doctor had come in, bringing with him a small, dark man whom he introduced as Luigi Romano. Brancati told his brokers that he might be transferring funds from his account to this man in the future. So naturally, when the executives received Brancati's letter, they immediately acted in accordance with their client's wishes.

Police followed the trail of Luigi Romano's money to a bank. Yes, the bankers said, Romano had deposited the total amount. No, they said, the money wasn't here any longer. You see, they said, Romano had waited a few weeks, then drawn out most of it, leaving around two hundred dollars.

So far, the police couldn't prove that anything illegal had happened. But, since they still half suspected kidnapping, they asked federal authorities for help in finding Brancati, and the information they received from this source made the kidnapping theory much less important.

Brancati, federal authorities said, had a record dating back to 1923, when he had been arrested as the leader of a ring of counterfeiters. What's more, there were strong links between Dr. Charles Brancati and a man named Arnold Rothstein.

Arnold Rothstein had been one of Brancati's few friends. If any New York City policeman didn't immediately recognize the name Arnold Rothstein, it was probably because he knew the man under another alias. Mr. Big, The Brain, Mr. A., A. R., The Man To See,

The Man Uptown, The Big Bankroll — these were all names used by a notorious gambler and gangster. The Rothstein-Brancati connection opened another can of worms.

Police went over what they knew about Rothstein, probing for insights into Brancati's disappearance.

As a teen, Rothstein trained his phenomenal computerlike mind with the help of his best friend Nicky Arnstein. Nicky randomly tossed out numbers; Rothstein added, subtracted, multiplied, and divided. He instantly spit out the right answer every time. He practiced figuring odds for hours, and when he sat down for a hand of poker, his face was as calculatedly blank as his mind was busily calculating. He gambled his way into a fortune.

By 1928, when he was forty-six years old, Rothstein had branched out into more than card games. He now took a hand in more underworld business than any other gangster in New York, and his hand always came out clean. Arnold Rothstein *was* Mr. Big. He ruled all of Broadway and most of the rest of Manhattan, and he did it with the help of two weapons — one was money, the other, terror.

Most of the money came from various betting enterprises, some of which Rothstein handled on a nightly walk down Broadway. His chauffeur pulled the limousine over to the curb on 49th Street, and Rothstein emerged with $200,000 in his pockets. (He usually walked around with a roll of bills totaling at least this amount, hence "The Big Bankroll" alias.) He paced slowly from 49th Street down to 42nd Street and back. He placed bets during these well-known "regular business hours," and occasionally he paid off one. But most of the time he collected from the small-time hustlers who gathered along Broadway and waited for Rothstein.

In the late 1920s, Rothstein was said to be worth fifty million dollars in bank deposits alone; some of that money went to pay for $400 suits, $50 shoes, a couple of dozen apartments, and the high cost of fixing things.

Rothstein could fix anything, from the outcome of the 1919 World Series (which he bought for around $70,000) to judges and public officials (whom he never pressed for repayment in dollars because their favors were more valuable). If something couldn't be fixed with money, Rothstein relied on his other weapon — terror.

One of his employees was Jack "Legs" Diamond, a killer who was astonishingly good at his job. For example, when mobster Dutch Schultz started to move in on Rothstein's gambling interests, Rothstein said a word or two to Legs, and Legs went happily to work. He ruthlessly gunned down six of Schultz's gang in three short days.

If Legs was a good killer, he was also a highly efficient loan and bet collector.

Legs liked his work, and he also liked his boss.

And it was a good thing that Legs liked Rothstein because Rothstein was continually losing friends. He lost his friend Nicky Arnstein because Arnstein had to be set up to take the prison sentence on some bond robberies Rothstein himself had masterminded. And Brancati *was* a friend, federal authorities assured New York police. In fact, Brancati was more than a friend — he was a business associate. He had helped Rothstein set up a nationwide dope ring. Police wondered if Rothstein had "lost" yet another friend.

Not that it would matter much to Rothstein now because — just to complicate matters further — only weeks before Brancati disappeared, Rothstein had died. His death had to have a bearing on Brancati's disappearance, police thought, so they pored over what they knew of Rothstein's last days.

Rothstein had gone into a decline toward the end of 1928. His health slipped; his face was white and his hands shook. Formerly proud of his expensive clothes and natty appearance, Rothstein started to let himself go. He lost his touch at fixing things, his fabled luck turned sour. For the first time in his life, Mr. Big was losing bets.

In early September, he lost a big bet — a lot of dollars and a big slice of his reputation. It all happened because a couple of sharp California gamblers came to town and trounced him solidly in a poker game held in a luxurious suite at the Park Central Hotel. The game ran on and on, from September 8th through the 10th, and Rothstein bet heavily and lost.

"How much?" Rothstein asked, after the winnings and losses were toted up.

"Three hundred twenty thousand dollars."

That was impossible! Rothstein exploded from his chair and glared at the California gamblers. "You cheated!" he shouted.

They looked at him and laughed.

Laughed! Did they know who they were dealing with? Mr. Big — that's who! No one laughed at Mr. Big!

The California sharpies stopped laughing, but they went on waiting for Rothstein's payment.

"I'll pay off in a day or two," Rothstein snapped. "I don't carry that sort of dough under my fingernails!" He left, slamming the door behind him.

He was The Big Bankroll, and he was lying. The California gamblers knew it. They kept trying to collect in the days and weeks that followed.

"I don't pay off on fixed poker!" Rothstein said. He stubbornly refused to pay.

Whether it was a fixed game or not, what Rothstein was doing was welshing on a bet. The whole underworld knew *that!* It was a violation of underworld "law," and there were whispers that trouble was coming. It arrived on November 4, 1928, when Rothstein quit taking bets on the presidential election and went back to the Park Central Hotel for another poker game.

Half an hour later, a bellboy found him by the service entrance, his hands clamped to his stomach in a hopeless attempt to hold back gushing blood. Mr. Big was rushed to the hospital, but no one could help him, and Rothstein refused to name his killers.

If Brancati had taken part in the Rothstein murder, police knew it was highly possible that he was just another victim of just another Roaring Twenties gangland killing by now. Legs was, after all, still on the prowl.

Police asked themselves: Had Brancati run frantically for safety, only to be gunned down? Had his limp body been disposed of secretly?

Or had Branacti heard whispers of trouble gathering around Rothstein and thought it prudent to drop out of sight because of his ties with the gambler? Was he now successfully hiding behind another name?

Police felt that the mysterious Luigi Romano might be able to help answer these questions, and they mounted an international search to ferret him out. If they could find the short, dark man who had been introduced to Brancati's brokers, they might find Brancati himself.

That's what police thought, but it didn't work out that way. Dr. Charles Brancati was never found.

What happened to him?

No one knew, but the case was closed anyway.

Police felt strongly that Brancati had been involved somehow in Rothstein's murder, and that his disappearance was a result of that involvement. Dr. Charles Brancati was declared legally dead in January, 1932.

And Luigi Romano?

He was not declared legally dead because no one was completely sure that he had ever existed! No one reported him missing, and no more trace of him was ever found anywhere on earth than was found of Dr. Charles Brancati.

Judge Crater

It is a little before 8:00 P.M. in Manhattan on August 6, 1930.

The tall man walking west on 45th Street will soon become the center of one of the most celebrated missing persons investigations of all time, but he doesn't appear to be concerned about approaching danger as he minces along briskly, taking quick steps that seem much too short for his long legs.

In fact, he doesn't appear to be worried about anything at all this evening. He has pulled his Panama hat to a jaunty angle, and the pearl gray spats over his shoes are unspotted and spiffy. The white collar he put on that morning still looks freshly starched, even though the night is hot and muggy. (He always wore chokerlike old-fashioned collars to hide the long neck that connected his disproportionately small head to the rest of his body.)

The man was Judge Joseph Force Crater, and he looked as dashing and well-dressed that evening as he always did.

Judge Crater liked clothes. The double-breasted, green-striped brown suit he wore that August night had been chosen from the thirty or so custom-tailored suits hanging in the closet of his luxurious apartment at 40 Fifth Avenue.

Another thing Judge Crater liked was the theater. In fact, he was coming from the Arrow Theater Ticket Agency on Broadway as he walked west on 45th Street. He'd gone there to get a ticket for *Dancing Partners,* a show he'd seen in preview the month before in Atlantic City. (He'd taken a trip, had some fun, and multilated the tip of his right index finger when a car door smashed shut on it. His hand was still bothering him.)

The ticket agent at the Arrow didn't have a seat left; the evening's performance was sold out. But the judge was a good customer and a friend, so he said he'd try to find a ticket somewhere.

"I'll leave it at the Belasco Theater's box office," he said. "You can pick it up when you get there."

That suited Judge Crater.

"Curtain time is 8:40," the ticket agent

added, and that suited Judge Crater, too. He'd have time to walk to Billy Haas's restaurant for a quick dinner before he went on to the Belasco.

At the restaurant, the judge checked his hat and started toward a table. A friend, William Klein, saw him and asked Crater to sit with him and his date.

Klein was also an attorney. He worked for the Shubert brothers, famous theatrical producers. His companion that night was Sally Lou Ritz, who had danced in a Shubert brothers show. Dinner conversation was sure to be about show business, one of Crater's favorite subjects. He sat with the couple, glad to put aside for the moment his own much more serious career.

Four months earlier, forty-one-year-old Crater had been appointed to the bench of the New York State Supreme Court by Franklin D. Roosevelt, then governor of the state. It was only an interim appointment to finish the unexpired term of a justice who had retired, but Crater wanted to remain on the bench after the elections in the fall. He hoped he would win the fourteen-year term; his legal and political friends were sure he would. They felt Crater was headed for far greater things, and they predicted that Crater would one day sit on the bench of the United States Supreme Court.

That suited Judge Crater, too — extremely

well. He'd told his wife he wanted a position "by which I will be remembered."

That night Crater drank his usual cocktail — orange juice — and enjoyed his meal. In high spirits, he told Klein and Ritz about his plans for the rest of the summer. He was going to return to his lakeshore cabin in Maine in time for his wife Stella's birthday on August 9th. The Craters had spent most of the summer there, and they had three more weeks on the sunny beach before the judge had to come back to the city. August 25th was when his court reconvened.

Crater had such a good time over dinner that he was astonished when he checked his gold watch. It was 9:15. He'd missed the whole first act of *Dancing Partners*! When he rose hurriedly, saying he could still see the last act of the show, Klein and Ritz decided to leave, too. The three of them walked outside together and talked for a few minutes on the sidewalk. Then Crater hailed a cab, shook hands with Klein, and got in. He waved good-bye as the cab merged with the westbound traffic on 45th, heading for the Belasco and Judge Crater's waiting ticket.

That evening someone — a man — picked up the ticket. Perhaps it was Crater himself, and perhaps Crater actually saw the show, but no one knows for sure.

Because no one ever saw Crater again to ask him.

On a hot, muggy August night in 1930, Judge Joseph Force Crater vanished totally and completely.

The search for him started quietly. His wife Stella was the first to wonder where he was. Four hundred miles away in their summer home in Maine, she waited for him to return for her birthday, as he had promised he would.

But when August 9th came and went and he didn't show up, Mrs. Crater grew anxious. She remembered things — mysterious things, like the telephone call her husband had received on the evening of Sunday, August 3rd, just before he left Maine to return to New York City. Who called him and what was said she didn't know, but she knew that the judge had started to pack as soon as he put down the receiver.

"I've got to straighten those fellows out," he said as he threw clothes into a suitcase.

They didn't discuss it any further; they never discussed the judge's business. The next morning, when he boarded the Bar Harbor Express for New York, he left the family car and the chauffeur, Fred Kahler, behind.

Finally, Mrs. Crater was too worried to just wait alone in Maine any longer. She asked Kahler to go to the city and find out what had happened to her husband.

Kahler went, stopping first at the Fifth

Avenue apartment. The maid was there, and when Kahler asked where the judge was, she told him she hadn't seen him for a long time — not since August 4th when he'd returned to the city from Maine. She said that Crater had told her then that she could take some time off, that she didn't have to clean the apartment until August 7th. When she'd returned to work, the judge wasn't there and she thought he had probably gone back to Maine. Was there a problem? she asked Kahler.

When Kahler wrote to tell Mrs. Crater this, she panicked and hired private detectives. They found nothing, so she telephoned the judge's business friends. They told her not to worry. Sometimes Crater left for a week or two, and with the November elections coming up, it wouldn't do to stir up any unfavorable publicity. Wait a few days, Crater's friends told his wife. He'll turn up by August 25th. He won't neglect his duties on the bench. He's too serious about work.

The judge's friends were right about his feeling for hard work. Even when he was a boy, Joe Crater wanted to be a judge, and he worked hard to get there. He graduated at the top of his high school class and won a full scholarship to Lafayette College. By the time he finished there in 1910, the Crater family fortune had dwindled, and Joe had had to tutor other students and apply for student loans to work his way through Columbia University's Law School. But he did it, taking his degree in 1913 and then working hard writing briefs for other lawyers in Manhattan. All the time his eyes were pinned on his life's goal — a seat on the Supreme Court of the United States.

Hardworking Joseph Crater came to the attention of Robert Ferdinand Wagner, a New York Supreme Court justice whose son would one day become mayor of New York City. Crater looked exceptionally promising, Wagner thought, and he hired him to act as his personal secretary in 1920.

That brought Crater to the attention of powerful city politicians. He soon became president of the prestigious Cayuga Democratic Club in the Nineteenth Assembly District. He held that position for ten years, all the time gaining allies and friends in Tammany Hall, the political machine that ruled the city.

Crater grew rich, making as much as $75,000 to $100,000 a year. He was named assistant professor at Fordham and New York universities and was a popular lecturer while still keeping up his heavy schedule of legal work. Now married to Stella, he moved his wife and himself into their plush Fifth Avenue apartment. He bought their summer home at Belgrade Lakes in Maine.

When he heard about the empty seat on the New York State Supreme Court, he went after it. The post paid only $22,500 — a quarter of his income — but he pulled every string he could until he got it.

That's why the judge's friends told his anxious wife not to worry. Crater would be there before the court session convened on the 25th, they said; Mrs. Crater could count on that!

But the judge's friends were wrong.

August 25th came and went, and court sessions opened without Judge Crater presiding.

On August 27th, a Supreme Court justice called a meeting of all the judges. Upset when Crater didn't appear, he telephoned Mrs. Crater in Maine, demanding an explanation. Now frantic, she told him the whole story.

On September 3rd — almost a full month after Crater disappeared — the story broke in the newspapers. The next day, one of Crater's friends went to the police, confirmed the story, and asked for help in finding him.

The Missing Person's Bureau responded immediately. They opened their famous File #13595 and began their investigation. And what officials uncovered was so shocking that it catapulted Judge Crater into the ranks of the most famous of missing persons!

He had wanted to be remembered, and he would be — although maybe not precisely in the way he dreamed of. (For example, for years nightclub comedians were sure they'd get a laugh with a line like, "Judge Crater, call your office.") Other people had vanished before; other *judges* had disappeared. But Judge Crater was different.

Judge Crater was a crook.

Crater had been living expensively for several years, and to pay for it, he'd dealt himself into more and more shady deals. The one that caught the public's attention involved Libby's Hotel on the Lower East Side of New York. The city condemned the twelve-story brick building. Crater took legal control of it during the proceedings and managed it for five months before it was sold to a private company for $75,000. Then, only two months later, the hotel was sold again to the City of New York — for the incredibly high price of $2,850,000! Officials said the city would destroy the hotel to make way for a street-widening project, but the project was never begun.

The Libby's Hotel deal came to symbolize the way Tammany Hall politicians swindled the public. The more people thought about it, the more they wondered what else Judge Joseph Force Crater was mixed up in. People who had never heard of Judge Crater before were now avidly interested in what had happened to him.

The police investigation wore on. They couldn't uncover any real clues that would solve the mystery of Crater's disappearance, but they discovered plenty to confuse and disorient their search. The judge had behaved strangely just before he vanished, and there was no telling what it all meant!

Again and again, investigators reconstructed the last few days of Judge Crater's life:

Sunday, August 3, 1930. Crater received his mysterious phone call in Maine. "I've got to straighten those fellows out," he said to his wife as he threw clothes into a suitcase.

Monday, August 4, 1930. In New York City, the judge told his maid not to come back until August 7th. Supposedly still on vacation, he went to his office and attended to routine business. Rather than making any obvious moves to "straighten those fellows out," Crater took the time to write a letter to a niece at a girls' camp. He ate lunch. He visited a doctor in Greenwich Village, saying he wanted to check his damaged finger.

Tuesday, August 5, 1930. Crater again spent most of the day in his office. He ate lunch with another judge. He ate dinner with the same doctor he had seen the day before, staying to play cards until 12:30 A.M.

A curious event took place on Tuesday, although Judge Crater may not have known about it. A woman appeared in the office of another attorney to see about filing a $100,000 lawsuit against Judge Crater. The attorney told the woman she didn't have a case, and the woman left, never to be heard from again.

Wednesday, August 6, 1930. On the day he

would disappear, Crater rose at 9:00 A.M. and dressed. Perhaps because the day was already warm, he didn't wear a vest. And perhaps the lack of vest pockets caused him to leave behind some prized possessions — his monogrammed pocket watch, pen, card case — when he left for his office.

By 11:00 A.M., the judge was at work, although he didn't seem to be dealing with routine tasks. His door was locked, and he was frantically pulling stacks of papers from his confidential files.

He called Joseph Mara, his attendant, and sent him out to cash two personal checks at different banks. When Mara returned with envelopes containing $5,150 in large bills, Crater snatched them hurriedly, stuffing them into his coat pocket without bothering to check or count the contents as he usually did.

Throughout the morning, Crater continued to pack his documents feverishly. When he had filled six expanding cardboard folders and his own briefcase, he called his secretary and borrowed another briefcase.

Shortly after noon, Crater called Mara again and asked him to help carry the carefully sealed papers outside to a cab. Neither Mara nor the secretary saw what papers the judge packed.

As he left, Crater made a point of telling his secretary to lock his office tightly.

Mara helped haul the documents to the judge's apartment. When all the papers were deposited on a chair, Crater turned to Mara and spoke slowly and distinctly, as if he were giving a lecture in a university or a summation in court. "You may go now, Joe. I'm going up Westchester way for a swim. I'll see you tomorrow."

Mara thought that was odd. The judge wasn't athletic; he hated swimming. A few minutes later, Mara left the apartment, and no one saw Crater the rest of the day.

When he walked into the Arrow Theater Ticket Agency in the early evening, he seemed to be the same as always. To William Klein and Sally Ann Ritz, Crater appeared to be in high spirits as he ate dinner and enjoyed show business chatter.

What happened to Judge Crater that afternoon to change his frantic mood into a high-spirited one?

Even more important, what happened to Judge Crater after he climbed into the cab, waved good-bye, and disappeared from the face of the earth?

A month later, when police were called into the case at last, they sent more than 10,000 circulars with a detailed description of Crater to police chiefs and sheriffs across the country and to foreign consulates. Detectives scoured city streets and the adjoining countryside looking for the missing judge. They found nothing.

The judge's apartment was inspected closely for any clues that might lead to the missing man, but everything was in perfect order.

New York City taxi drivers were questioned and their trip tickets were checked. Crater was a well-known figure; a cab driver would have remembered Judge Crater! But there was no trace of a trip ticket to the Belasco Theater, and no one came forward to boast that he had driven Crater on the night in question.

Rewards totaling $7,500 were posted.

Three hundred persons were interviewed.

Thousands of telegrams and letters arrived.

Depositions were taken.

A grand jury was called to look into the case, and it struggled through the 2,000 typewritten pages of testimony taken during forty-five sessions.

Nothing.

The police tried another idea. The documents Crater took from his office so furtively the day he disappeared were never found, but a close search of Crater's remaining files might tell them what was missing. They checked painstakingly. That didn't help. What Judge Crater took from his office remained a secret.

Then maybe, police thought, Mrs. Crater had something to tell investigators. She didn't. She was willing to tell what she knew, but she simply didn't know anything about the judge's business since they never talked about it.

She suffered a nervous collapse in Maine, then recovered and came to New York City at the end of January. And the minute Mrs. Crater looked around the Fifth Avenue apartment, she made an astonishing discovery. At last there was a clue — a manila envelope, which the judge had addressed to Mrs. Crater, was hidden in a secret drawer of her bedroom dresser!

Impossible, said police, who had searched the apartment and found the secret drawer themselves. The only difference was that when they saw it, the drawer was empty.

The contents of the envelope were even more surprising than the envelope itself. There was money — cash, checks, records of debts owed the judge, stock certificates, bonds, and several insurance policies on Crater's life worth thousands of dollars. All of this would go to Mrs. Crater, according to a will the judge had written five years earlier.

But most surprising of all was a three-page note addressed to Stella, supposedly from Crater.

The handwriting of the undated note seemed strange, as if it had been written by someone under a lot of pressure. It was scribbling, really, with ragged margins and lots of abbreviations. The note listed twenty-one people who owed Crater money.

The regular legal fees from the Libby's Hotel deal were owed, as well as a great deal more. The note read: "There will be a large sum due me for services when the city pays the 2¾ million in condemnation. Martin Lippman will attend to it — keep in touch with him." (Lippman and every other debtor Crater listed would later deny that they owed the judge anything.)

At the bottom of the note was written. *"This Is All Confidential.* I am very wary. Love, Joe."

The police didn't believe it. The note had to have been written before September 10, 1930, because one of the debts listed mentioned a repayment expected on that date. The envelope had to have been delivered to the locked apartment — either by Crater or someone he trusted — after his disappearance and *after* the police searched the apartment on September 4, 1930. Even more mysteriously, three of the checks in the envelope were dated August 30, 1930 — three weeks after the judge vanished!

All these items were the sort of documents usually placed in safety deposit boxes, which can only be opened by authorized persons. The mystery deepened when the judge's safety deposit box was examined. Amazingly, it was empty!

Police asked themselves if Stella had somehow found the key to the safety deposit box, removed the contents, and placed them where they could be conveniently found. She had every reason to do so; she would gain a great deal.

Or had someone else done it? If so, why? Had the safety deposit box been opened by Crater himself, still concerned about his wife's welfare? Was he alive? And, if so, where was he?

Many answers to this question have been offered, most of them pointing to the same conclusion — Judge Crater had been murdered.

One of these theories centered around the money from the Libby's Hotel deal. Crater had been in on the deal, and he expected a share of the immense profits. But other people were in on the deal, too, and if Crater were done away with, those other people wouldn't have to split with him. Their profits would be even greater.

Another murder theory was offered by Crater's sister. She thought that Crater was the victim of a criminal who swore to "get" Crater as he was being taken off to prison. When the criminal was freed, he carried through on his threat.

Still another murder theory revolved around the judge's Tammany Hall companions in shady deals. According to this theory, the judge sifted through his files to find documents that would incriminate his cronies. Then he kept his date with "those fellows" in Westchester, and they decided to keep him quiet forever.

Yet another murder plot cast Judge Crater

as the victim of blackmail. A show girl — perhaps the same one who visited an attorney about pressing Crater with a lawsuit hours before he disappeared — called Crater to a meeting somewhere. When he wouldn't do what she wanted, her friends tried to "persuade" the judge by beating him, and they hit too hard.

Years later, the murder theories gained spectacular support. A journalist went to Dutch psychic Gerary Croiset, who had solved many crimes for the police in the Netherlands. Croiset, merely by touching the back of a photograph of Crater, was able to describe many details of the events known to surround the man's disappearance. In a trance, the psychic said. "This man is not alive . . . he was murdered long ago. . . ." Then he described a burial site in the area of Westchester, and that astonishing fact was corroborated by secret police information!

Investigators rushed to dig up the likely places. No trace of Crater's body was found.

Other people agree that Crater died, but they think it was a natural death. They say his body was hidden by his Tammany Hall associates — "those fellows" — to avoid scandal. Crater's heart was bad, these people claim, and they point to information that surfaced during the judge's trip to Atlantic City a month before he disappeared. A companion on that trip — the same ticket agent who found the judge a seat for *Dancing Partners*

— said that Crater went swimming, but soon left the ocean, complaining of chest pains.

Add to this that Crater visited a doctor twice during the first two days after he returned to New York from Maine, saying he wanted his mashed finger looked after. Oddly enough, he did not visit his usual physician. According to information from Mrs. Crater, the judge went to an old friend instead.

Had Crater suspected he was seriously ill? Had he consulted a doctor he could trust to be discreet because he didn't want to worry his wife or his political friends?

If so, could bad health — a bad heart — have resulted in the judge's death? Did he go to Westchester to talk with "those fellows," as some people suggest, only to suffer a fatal heart attack in the heat of the discussion? And was his body then buried in a well-hidden grave by political cronies, who were happy to let the judge just "disappear"?

It's possible, but no one can be sure now.

Other explanations advance the idea that the judge *himself* decided to disappear.

One close friend said she knew the judge was tired of working so hard, tired of the political in-fighting it took to maintain his position. She said that he told her that his "idea of being at peace with the world, complete, everlasting peace, is to go into a monastery and never come out again." The last time Crater saw her, he said, "I feel that I've already quit the world. . . . Don't try to drag me back."

Many of the police officers who worked on the Crater case agree that the man's disappearance was premeditated. He may have entered a monastery, they say, but it's more likely that a tough-minded political pro like Joe Crater could sense the winds of reform blowing against the Tammany Hall machine. He could see an investigation coming, and he got out before they could get him.

Where he went and what happened to him, these officers won't guess, but they point out that Crater withdrew large amounts of money and placed them in foreign banks during the months before he vanished, as if he were preparing for a new life.

File #13595 of the New York Police Department's Missing Persons Bureau remains open today, a standing memorial to one of the most baffling of all the cases they have ever investigated. The file bulges with information about the Crater case — tips and clues and reports — but it does not contain an answer to the question: What happened to Judge Joseph Force Crater?

Johnny Gosch

September 5, 1982, was a warm Sunday morning, and twelve-year-old Johnny Gosch woke before six o'clock. The rest of his family was still asleep in their West Des Moines home as Johnny tugged on cut-offs and a white T-shirt and sandals. In fact, most of the people who lived in the suburban Iowa neighborhood were still sleeping as he called his small dog Gretchen, got his wagon, and left home to pick up his bundle of newspapers.

Johnny had a paper route for a little less than a year, but his thirty-seven customers felt they could count on him. His boss felt that way, too: "He's got a good record — good service record, good collecting record, good sales record. He happens to do a good job."

As Johnny approached the paper drop on the corner of 42nd Street and Ashworth Road, a man driving a dark blue car pulled up. He turned off the car lights and slid over to the passenger's side of the seat to stop Johnny and ask him for directions to 86th Street. Johnny spoke to him, but the man couldn't seem to understand. Finally, Johnny gave up and went on to the paper drop, leaving the man sitting in his car. The man spun a U-turn and followed. They spoke again at the paper drop, then the dark blue car tore off east on Ashworth.

Johnny dumped his papers into his wagon, talked with another carrier, and started off on his route. He parked his wagon at the corner of 42nd and Marcourt Lane, a short block from where he'd loaded it, and sat in it, getting ready to undo the bundle of papers. He usually left his wagon on this corner while he delivered to nearby subscribers.

A few minutes later, someone who lived near that corner saw a silver Ford Fairmont with a wide black stripe on the side, but he saw no sign of Johnny Gosch.

In the space of a few, short minutes, Johnny Gosch had vanished.

It wasn't long before his disappearance was noticed. At 7:45, a customer telephoned the Gosch home to ask why her paper hadn't been delivered. She was surprised. Johnny's father, who took the call, was surprised, too. After he hung up, he went to his son's room and found the bed empty. Johnny hadn't overslept. Or at least if he had, he was gone now — probably out making those deliveries.

But then Johnny's father noticed something odd. Johnny's dog was home. If his son were out on his paper route, why wasn't Gretchen with him as usual?

Too many things were just a little different that morning, and they were beginning to add up to some uncomfortably nagging questions for Johnny's parents. Mr. and Mrs. Gosch decided to check along their son's route. They found the loaded wagon a couple of blocks from home. The bundle was unbroken, none of the papers had been delivered, and there was no sign of Johnny. If he were pulling some sort of prank, he probably would have delivered his papers first, not only because he was a responsible and dependable paperboy, but also because carriers were charged 75¢ for each undelivered paper. It would have to have been a terrific prank to cause Johnny to fork over the $27.75 it would cost him. No, it didn't feel right. . . .

At 8:30 Johnny's parents called the police, who responded at once. An officer spoke to the handful of people who had last seen the missing boy.

Paper carriers told them the man in the dark blue car had been driving around the area for about a half hour before he stopped Johnny. They described the man as being in his mid-30s and weighing about two hundred pounds. He had dark features and a mustache, and he was wearing a baseball cap. He seemed upset and disgusted, and his eyes were wide and beady. From descriptions of the mystery man in the baseball cap, a police artist drew a sketch.

When the mystery man drove from the paper drop, one witness glanced at the license plate on his car. Later, under hypnosis, this witness was able to tell police that the car was licensed in Warren County, south of Des Moines. He also recalled several of the numbers on the license plate.

One of the witnesses said he saw a man emerge from the early morning shadows and talk to Gosch as he pulled his loaded wagon up 42nd Street. This man wasn't wearing a baseball cap, and Johnny hadn't seemed frightened. Gretchen wasn't barking either, so there hadn't seemed to be any danger.

Police talked to the carrier who had seen Johnny sit in his wagon at 42nd and Marcourt and to the man who had seen the silver car at the corner where the wagon was parked — without Johnny — only moments later. Then they called over twenty-five law enforcement officers from various departments and agencies into the search for Johnny Gosch on the Sunday he disappeared.

Dozens of family friends and neighbors spent the day helping, too. They were stopped by a drenching afternoon shower, but resumed the hunt later and kept at it until darkness fell. Johnny was not found.

Monday dawned. Over a thousand people of all ages turned out to spend the last of their Labor Day holiday searching. Some of them gathered at nearby South Woods Park, where they were organized into lines and told not to trample or touch anything: "You're just here to walk and look." The lines of searchers moved out, walking through the tall grass, which was damp from the previous day's rain. They brushed aside clouds of autumn gnats and mosquitoes and looked for a yellow newspaper bag, a baseball cap, or any of the clothes Johnny had been wearing.

Other volunteers drove slowly along the rural roads on the west edge of the city, straining to catch sight of the same objects — signs of a missing boy or of anyone who might have information needed to find him. Still other people scouted urban streets, looking for two cars — the dark blue vehicle driven by the mystery man in the baseball cap or the the silver, black-striped Ford Fairmont. The newspaper for which Johnny worked offered a reward of $5,000 "for information leading to the whereabouts of John Gosch." But as Monday came to an end, his whereabouts remained a mystery.

On Tuesday, one hundred volunteers, some of them on horseback, advanced through other wooded areas: Walnut Woods, Hoak Road, Greenbelt Park, the banks of the Raccoon River. Police called on Greta Alexander, a psychic from Illinois who had been helpful in solving past cases of missing persons. They also continued their usual investigative methods, such as interviewing neighbors, relatives, friends, students, teachers, and staff members at centers for runaways. Saying they thought the mystery man was probably a passing drunk, police decided against releasing their artist's sketch. They put out another call for information about the two cars, and asked the drivers, whom they said were not considered suspects, to come forward and share what they knew. Schools were back in session after the holiday, but Johnny Gosch's seat in seventh grade at Indian Hills Junior High School was empty, and the school principal noted an anxious feeling in the building.

Johnny's seat was empty on Wednesday, too, while Iowa State Patrol planes flew aerial searches, and while volunteers and law enforcement officers investigated fields and farms and old empty buildings. A few days after Johnny vanished, police received a report of a large pool of blood in a stall of a coin-operated car wash. But the blood was a different blood type than Johnny's, and police said that that report, tips from other sources, and a close check of all-night establishments that might supply a clue to the boy's whereabouts were all leading to the same place — nowhere.

On Thursday, the reward fund climbed to $33,000. Aerial searches continued. Police focused their interest on an unexpected area of central Iowa, around the small towns of Adair, Atlantic, and Anita. What had directed them there? The police weren't saying, but some people believed they were following up on information given them by the psychic.

As the first week of Johnny's absence drew to a close, no trace of him had come to light and no new clues had surfaced, but some different information had appeared with the reward offer that the newspaper was running. Johnny Gosch may have been wearing shorts and a T-shirt when he disappeared, as earlier reports said, or he could have been wearing black sweatpants and a white pullover with "Kim's Academy" lettered in black on the back. His parents weren't sure since they hadn't seen him when he left the house early Sunday morning. The physical description of the boy remained the same, however — 5'7" and 140 pounds. And where he was also remained the same — unknown.

The weeks wore on. The Gosches had gotten in touch with a psychic of their own in the first hours following Johnny's disappearance, and later they hired a private detective. They talked about their missing son on a national television show. They had handbills and posters printed with information about him, and a huge mailing went out with the help of many volunteer staplers and folders.

But by November 12th, Johnny's thirteenth birthday, nothing had panned out.

Both official and private searchers failed to produce anything.

As Thanksgiving Day approached, the Gosches had spent their entire savings in efforts to find their son. They asked volunteers to help raise money for the Find Johnny Gosch Fund by selling chocolate bars in booths at shopping malls. Help Find Johnny Gosch Inc., a nonprofit volunteer organization, would handle the money.

Then, in the last days of November, the Gosches held a surprise press conference. They released the sketch of the man in the baseball cap they had asked a private artist to draw, saying they were confident this man was the key to unlocking the mystery of Johnny's disappearance. Their private detective pointed to a remark Johnny made three months earlier to another newspaper carrier on the corner of 42nd and Ashworth. Johnny said the man in the blue car was weird. *Weird* is a word that can have many meanings, but words can be significant — especially last words.

The Christmas season began, and Johnny Gosch didn't reappear, even though the search had widened. The Des Moines *Register* sent hundreds of letters to newspapers throughout the United States and Canada, asking them to print a small notice with Johnny's picture, and at least 150 of the papers did. HBO (cable TV) camera crews had filmed a search of Walnut Woods for a documentary on missing children to be aired later. The booths in the shopping malls continued to sell candy.

Then, on December 22, 1982, there seemed to be a break in the case. "We'll have Johnny home for Christmas," Mrs. Gosch said happily. She and her family said they wouldn't celebrate Christmas until Johnny was home to share it. The Gosches reported that their private investigator had found information that led them to believe Johnny was alive and somewhere in central Iowa. The next day they announced they had found a man who claimed to have seen Johnny *after* he vanished from his paper route!

Police weren't so sure that the man was the key to the puzzle. They offered their own reward — $1,000 each for information about the two suspicious cars seen by witnesses on the morning that Johnny disappeared.

Christmas came and went. Johnny Gosch didn't come home for the holidays. And when police interviewed the man the Gosches thought might be able to tell them what happened to their son, they shook their heads, telling reporters the man was a hoax. He'd telephoned the Gosches in late November and told them he'd picked up their son on the interstate about a half mile from where the boy was last seen. The man said he'd talked with Johnny as they drove along, and grown suspicious. Thinking he had a runaway on his hands, he stopped in the small town of

Atlantic, Iowa, to call the police. When he returned to his truck, he said, Johnny was gone.

Police said everything the man knew came from newspaper reports. Besides that, they had information proving the man was in Texas at the same time he claimed to have given Johnny a ride. The Gosches didn't agree. They said the man knew about an argument at school between Johnny and another student, something he could have learned only by talking to Johnny. The scuffle hadn't been reported in the papers, Johnny's parents hadn't mentiond it in their conversations with the man, and their private investigator hadn't been able to turn up any proof at all that the man was in Texas at the time in question!

Was the man a hoax? Why was he lying, if he was lying?

But the largest question — the one that loomed over all the others — was what happened to Johnny Gosch?

Did he run away from home? Thousands of kids run away every year — some authorities estimate the number to be as high as two *million* each year! — but most of them return in a couple of weeks. Johnny Gosch's parents and friends don't believe he ran away. He seemed to be happy, with no overpowering problems crowding his life.

Was he taken — kidnapped? His parents believe this is what had happened, even though there was no evidence of foul play

133

near his abandoned wagon, and no ransom note ever arrived. The police psychic reportedly felt a sense of struggle during the first days following Johnny's disappearance; several days later, she had the sense of confinement, of being tied up.

Did the man in the baseball cap take Johnny? Or set him up for the other man, the one who stepped from the early morning shadows? Was Johnny the victim of a kidnapping partnership?

By the time six months passed, nearly eighty people who claimed to have special, supernatural knowledge tried to solve the mystery of his disappearance. A year later, the number had risen to two hundred. All of them failed to find a trace of Johnny Gosch.

Police tried every avenue of investigation. They checked the registrations of hundreds of cars, trying to find the two seen in the area at the right time. They called in the Des Moines police and the Polk County sheriff's office and other official agencies to help find Ford Fairmont owners throughout the state. They didn't find a trace of repainting or of a change of registration, both of which could have been proof of a "borrowed" vehicle. And they didn't find a trace of Johnny Gosch.

Both police and private investigators continued doggedly to follow up leads from people who thought they had seen the missing boy. There have been many.

Shortly after Johnny disappeared two separate calls from Toronto, Ontario, Canada, came to nothing.

About three months after Johnny disappeared, police in Cedar Grove, New Jersey, responded to missing persons bulletins and said they had a young "John Doe" who had been beaten and was unable to talk and identify himself. ("John Doe" is a name given to unidentified people.) But the New Jersey boy didn't have blue eyes or a birth mark on his chest; Johnny Gosch was still missing.

Six months after his disappearance, the Iowa Division of Criminal Investigation had handled at least one hundred such reports of possible sightings or identifications of Johnny Gosch, one of them involving a startled boot salesman in a campground in Nebraska who had been "identified" as the imprisoner of a boy who looked like Johnny. When his recreational vehicle was searched, only a lot of boot samples were found.

At about the same time, Johnny Gosch was "seen" in a pizza parlor in Arlington, Texas, but the FBI couldn't find him through that lead.

Nine months after he disappeared, the body of a teenaged stabbing victim in Illinois was found. It wasn't Johnny.

The list could go on and on, but none of the sightings has answered the question of what happened to Johnny Gosch.

The fact is he's gone, and whether he ran away or was stolen, when Johnny Gosch disappeared, he joined the ranks of missing children, a huge group that continues to grow each year.

Parents of missing children say the worst problem they face is uncertainty — not knowing what happened, hoping that nothing deadly did, and waiting for news. "Somewhere around two or three in the morning, the eyeballs pop open and there we are thinking of our son," said Johnny Gosch's mother. Yet there's always hope — because there *are* homecomings. For most families, the hope of one person is enough reason to keep up the search for a missing family member for years. The families can turn to organizations like Child Find or Search, and descriptions of missing children can now be entered in the FBI's National Crime Information Computer. But ultimately, the solution to many of these missing young persons mysteries is simply waiting and not giving up hope.

Police go on record saying that they have a "gut feeling" that Johnny Gosch is still alive. They've worked hard for months without finding a trace of Johnny's remains, so there's a good chance he is alive, especially since the National Unidentified Dead file, organized and maintained by the Colorado Bureau of Investigation in Denver, has no unclaimed body that matches Johnny Gosch's description.

And there's more to add to the Gosches' hope that Johnny is still alive. More than nine months after he disappeared, there were nine separate sightings of a young man who matches Johnny's description. All the sightings placed Johnny in the company of a pair of truckers — one white, one black — driving an unmarked semi. A spokesperson for the family told reporters that these sightings came from people in widely spread states — Florida, Georgia, Mississippi, Louisiana, Texas, Oregon, and Washington.

Is Johnny Gosch still alive? Will he come home?

No one knows any more than they know what happens to the hundreds of thousands of young people who vanish every year.

For the Gosches, like many other parents, the answer to the mystery is simply waiting, and putting off the day when they must say, as Johnny Gosch's mother puts it, "Johnny, we're going to have to give up."